ST. AUSTELL SPEEDWAY
1958-1963
Plus The Sidecar Years

J & S Publications,
Glen Maye,
85,Park Way,
Fairfield Park,
St.Austell,
PL25 4HR.
Tel.01726-66484.
www.booksmotorcycling.org.uk

A catalogue record for this book is available from the British Library.
ISBN: 978-0-942641-97-4

Design and Typesetting by Louise Hillier Designs, St.Agnes. Tel.01872 554490.

Printed in Cornwall, England by MPG Books Ltd.

CONTENTS

INTRODUCTION

A Cornishman by the name of Chris Harris has put Speedway racing in Britain back in the public domain. Harris has done for speedway what Amir Khan has done for Boxing. The Team Great Britain star, who rides for the Coventry Bees in the Elite League never fails to give 101% effort. In 2007 Harris scooped the British Individual Speedway Championship, and was the winner of the British Speedway Grand Prix at the Millennium Stadium, Cardiff. The author has watched Chris' progress since he was fourteen years of age and is delighted to highlight his success in the local press.

Chris 'Bomber' Harris will probably be one of the first people to receive a copy of this book and have Jeremy's nomination for Sports Personality of the Year.

Motorcycles have been used in the Westcountry since the early part of the twentieth century. The highly competitive grass-speedway was seen around the Duchy of Cornwall since the early thirties, racing at Rocky Park often boasted crowds of over five thousand spectators. Jeremy Jackson, who documented Cornish track racing in the book 'St. Austell Speedway, the Early Years 1949-1954', gave the reader an in depth nostalgic look back at the most southerly shale track in the U.K. It is hard to believe but this era brought in huge crowds of up to 18,000 spectators.

Jeremy's book 'The Early Years' was launched in May 2006 at a special 'Speedway Memories' evening at Trewoon Village Hall near St.Austell. The evening which was tinged with nostalgia was heralded a great success and raised a sum of £862-15 for Cornwall Hospice Care. Jeremy has also signed books at St.Boniface Arena, Plymouth and at Asda Stores in Cromwell Road, St.Austell on St.Pirans Day.

'Jerry' as he prefers to be called has been around motorcycles since he was seventeen years old. The motorcycle seed was probably sown as a youngster with tales of his late Dad riding British built police motorcycles. As a teenager he supported sidecar ace Phil Williams and travelled the country with him. His first excursion into print was about ice racer Bruce Semmonds, he has written several books since the mid-nineties including three 'Champions' editions and Len Read's biography. He was a member of the track staff at the Claycountry Moto-Parc in 1997 pushing off bikes with his friend Len Keast. Although 'Jerry' is a keen motorcyclist he has never had the ambition to ride in speedway but has been inspired to put pen to paper by the courage, heroics and quest of track riders 'to lay it on the line to be the best'. Jerry has watched speedway at few tracks around the U.K. including St.Austell, Plymouth, Exeter, Ipswich, Coventry and at Cardiff.

This is the sequel book in which 'Jerry' highlights the ups and downs of the sport at Par Moor. The Cornish Stadium became the training ground of just a few of the future stars of the sport. The writer makes no apology for his style of narrative and frank use of anecdotes. He was fully aware it was Trevor Redmond who breathed life back into speedway, which was in decline during that period. As the author points out: 'Without Trevor Redmond we may not have seen Brian Annear resurrect the sport at the Claycountry Moto-Parc some thirty four years later.'

'Jerry' is thoroughly imbued with the spirit of his subject and keeps intrinsic the social events of the time. This book has the results, but more importantly the precious memories from people who enjoyed going to watch speedway. Also for those of you who enjoyed watching the charioteers, we meet the sidecar boys down the years. They have their glimpse of action under the floodlights too. As Jackson explains: 'Speedway became part of their way of life. Being proud of my Cornish heritage I think I can say I delved deep with my research to establish how St.Austell Speedway evolved into one of the friendliest clubs, in one of the most beautiful parts of the country, so do enjoy your trip down memory lane!'

ACKNOWLEDGEMENTS

To plot the ups and downs of the Par Moor track would have been impossible without the generous help, support and advice of several like-minded friends. My sincere thanks goes to everyone concerned. I would like to say 'thank you' to all these wonderful people, although they are not listed in any particular order: Terry Knight and the team at the Cornish Studies Library in Redruth, Royal Cornwall Museum, Cornwall Record Office, Stuart Johnson, Ivan Mauger M.B.E. O.B.E., Fred Paul, Walter Dawson, Tony Lethbridge, Eric Martyn, Margaret Tucker, Valerie Cann, Mrs.Biddy Mitchell, Andrew Eddy, Terence Eddy, John Payton, Ken Westaway, Robert Peareth, Francis Cantell, Ray Sparks, Reg Bazely, Derek Frost, John Luke, Tony Oxford, Malcolm Ball, Ivor Toms, Rosemary Williams, Ken Richards, Vic Morris, Bill Uren, Ken Hicks, Dave Saunby, Mike Tremayne, Ivor Menear, John Jarvis, Glyn Chandler, George Major, Ray Cresp, John Somerville, Les Nicholas, Jim Henry, John Yeo, Jack Gates, David Stephens, Alan Martin, Dave Stallworthy, Crispen Rosevear, Neil Truran, Guy Redmond, Martin Rogers, Colin Martin, John Brownhill, Robin Hendry, and Andrew Wedlake.

Regrettably, many of my friends are no longer with us, but they also made contributions however small, including Ron Bassett, Eric Abbot, Ken Tucker, Phil Williams, Ian Mitchell, Goog Hoskin, Ray Wickett, Roy Wedlake, Francis Cann and Eddie Seymour.

I am also indebted to Speedway Star and News, Vintage Speedway Magazine, Stenners, and the Speedway Researcher for statistical information. On the subject of photographs I have tried hard to give the correct accreditation, if any of your's were unmarked we humbly apologise for any inconvenience caused.

Again, a thank you to my immediate family, to my wife Shirley, my daughter Julie and her husband Karl. Sometimes they took phone calls, on other

Most speedway and track rider's are daredevils, they have no fear. Sometimes age has no barrier, local star Adrian Kessell started riding in September 1945, today he is still competing. Likewise George Craig who rode at St.Austell and Plymouth in the early fifties is still very active at over ninety years of age. Here the Australian is seen making his 900th skydiving jump on his 90th birthday. Ivor Toms did several free fall jumps for charity including one into Cornish Stadium, as he descended he could see the marker on the centre field but ended up landing in the Britannia Inn car park.

occasions they not only made the tea but put up with me enthusiastically rambling on, sometimes about people they had never heard of!

Finally, without Louise Hillier the book designer who added her magic touch to the typeset, Glynn Shailes for the first proof reading, Roger Fogg for typing his valued memories, Rob Bamford for his statistical assistance, and Colin Rugg for years of background support, this book would not have become a reality. I cannot believe we have produced nine books in twelve years. With your support there may be others.

1958
A return to open licence speedway

The county of Cornwall had been devoid of speedway at Par Moor for four years and many enthusiasts missed their weekly 'whiff of Castrol R'. However, some had been converted to the new sport of stock car racing, which first appeared on Tuesday 6 August 1955. It's popularity passed the test of time because it remained at the circuit for over thirty years, during which time many top drivers were nurtured and went on to enjoy national status. Do you remember the likes of British and World Champion Billy Batten from Newton Abbot or Liskeard's three times World Champion Dave Brown? How about former World Champion Jeremy Deeble or Plymouth's Dave Bunt?

Also, one must not forget Callington's Mike Williams, St.Austell's Mike James, Notter Bridge's Johnny Marquand or Dave Luscombe of Totnes. There were others of course, including Spence Morgan, former British Champion Colin Higman, George Coaker, Mike Brown and even Conroy Brown. Not forgetting Reg Hawken of Porthpean, who knew every turn of the track when it had a shale surface!

The pair who brought 'stock-car and banger-racing' into the limelight were New Zealand speedway international Trevor Redmond and his father-in-law Bob Netcott. Redmond, who was undoubtedly a unique showman, saw an opportunity to bring back speedway to the Duchy. Former track-staff pusher Ron Bassett who worked at John Williams Joinery, and his pals were eating their sandwiches outside one lunchtime when they were disturbed by Redmond himself. The Kiwi knew exactly where to find the people to spread the word. He explained to Ron and his friends that he wanted to bring speedway back, just for a short season. Redmond went to live with the 'House' family at 64, Clifden Road and undoubtedly enjoyed their warm hospitality, as had several other speedway riders before him. While staying in Clifden Road, Trevor got to know several local people on 'christian name terms'.

The lads at John Williams Joinery and Charlestown Engineering, who were both subsidiaries of E.C.L.P. (this abbreviation stood for English Clays Lovering and Pochin) together with the staff of several local garages enthused about the rebirth of their sport. So, with many of the former track-staff returning Messrs Redmond and Netcott must have sensed they were on a winner. They registered as joint promoters, running just a few meetings during the peak holiday season under an open licence.

The track-staff of this era included announcer Bill Dalley, and the public address support man Gerald Rowe, while the pit stewards were Charlie Lobb and W.J. Short. The timekeeper was T.C.E. Clapp, with Bob Netcott taking on the 'clerk of the course' role himself. The predominant A.C.U. steward was Mr.Freddie Vigers. Some of the other helpers, pushers and rakers are listed here: they were Jack Annear and his son Brian of Tywardreath Highway, Bill Martin and his son Larry of Par, plus Ron Bassett, Ross Edwards, Ray Ball, Robin Hendry, Walter Bovey, Mickey Luxon, John Luke, Derek Frost, Tom Bromley, Geoff Jarvis, Frank Bazeley, Terry Hodge, Ken Kent, Ron Phillips, Russell Masters, Wilfred Wakeham, Barbara French, John Ford and Jim Perryman who ran the public bar. Incidentally for those of you who didn't know Colonel Fitzroy Llewellyn was a pseudonym used by Bob Netcott.

Missing from the management team was the flamboyant 'Chirpy' Richards. Jerry went to meet Mrs.Biddy Mitchell(nee King) who was Chirpy's personal secretary, she explained why her boss was no longer involved in the shale sport. It appears business came first.

Biddy said, "Phillips and Geake moved to Beech Road in January 1954 and from that time on he worked all hours. He often worked twelve hours a day buying and selling vehicles, we had to fall in with him. When he ran the speedway he was good at booking star riders at the last minute, organising lodgings at the drop of a hat, and even sorting out transport. Chirpy had the contacts to make things happen, but he was good at delegation too. I think his trademark had to be his notebook, he had it at speedway and again at work." She described Chirpy as great chap but 'hard work!'

The author said, "It is no secret either that Trevor Redmond and Chirpy Richards did not get along."

Another person who knew Chirpy extremely well for over twenty years was Alan Grose because he went to school with A.D.Richards son, Keith. Alan who lived at 105 Slades Road has fond memories of watching speedway and 'banger racing'. He said he knew Roy Wedlake really well, and recalled him working on cars in Carclaze Road, and riding outfits 'on' and 'off' track. Alan recalled, "My Dad, Howard Grose, for many years owned Bethesda Farm off Cypress Avenue at Carlyon Bay and occasionally he was asked to come over to the track by the Luke family or Trevor Redmond to collect some banger wreckage. Dad would drive the Ferguson tractor over and tow back the badly wrecked car, which was then dumped down the mineshaft on his property. In the twenty first century the practice would be 'taboo' but in the sixties it happened." Incidentally, the rows of trees which flanked Cypress Avenue for decades have since been felled, and a new road improvement scheme has been implemented. Also a mineshaft had to be capped whilst constructing the Wheal Regent Estate at Carlyon Bay. Today, Alan lives in Indiana, alternating with his other U.S. property in Sebring, Florida. Also worth a mention, on a rare trip to the U.K. in 1994 Alan visited the charity bike show at Par Moor organized by the author.

In March 1958 the hip swiveling teen idol Elvis Presley was drafted into the U.S. Army for two years but his music still reverberated from the crackly trackside speakers at the Stadium.

Another milestone worthy of note was the first greyhound meeting, which took place at Par Moor on Friday 4 July. To protect the dog track, a bridge of wood planking was used whilst pushing the bikes to and from the pits. Incidentally the author's late uncle, Harry Williams of Troon raced greyhounds at Cornish Stadium for several years. Mr. Redmond commented to the local press: "We want to get the speedway on here every Wednesday. League fixtures are not usually held on Wednesdays so the best riders in the country are free on that day. There is no limit to the riders we can bring down."

Derek Frost, who worked for Par Engineering in 1958, drove the tractor for grading the track. He said: 'Par Engineering supplied the tractor, which I drove up until I got married. Financial constraints and family pressures always seemed to get in the way and I finally dropped the speedway off. I still saw some of the riders though, because they stayed with our family. My memory of this era was watching young riders like Chris Julian striking out in the sport.' Incidentally 'Par Engineering' just off Eastcliffe Road no longer exists, it was demolished to make way for new housing.

Today, Derek runs Cornish Coachways, which takes him to places far and wide. Occasionally, one of his passengers from the older generation may mention speedway, but they are becoming fewer all the time. Derek concluded that he so enjoyed watching the leg-trailers of the 1950s like Mick Mitchell. He also described the style of George Craig, who was perhaps a semi-trailer. Today, Craig lives in Medina, Western Australia, where he still enjoys skydiving at over 90 years of age!

The first meeting on Wednesday 30 July was the British League Best Pairs and the event was heralded a great success. The line-up included Australians Jack Young, Peter Moore and Ray Cresp, Southampton captain Dick Bradley and an 'up and coming rider' from the outskirts of Exeter, namely Francis Cann. Other riders were Ian Williams and Neil Street from Swindon, Johnny Hole of Southampton, and the Leicester pair of Jack Geran and Gerald Hussey. Completing the programme were Ronnie Genz and New Zealander Charlie New, who rode for Oxford. The meeting resulted in victory for Geran and Hussey, who between them accumulated 21 points. Thousands of people turned out to watch the sport return to Par Moor, although not quite as many as the inaugural meeting in 1949. Full result: Geran (12) and Hussey (9) = 21; Moore (15) and Cresp (3) = 18; Genz (10) and New (6) = 16; Bradley (10) and Hole (3) = 13; Young (13) and Cann (0) = 13; Williams (8) and Street (1) = 9; Chris Julian (reserve) 0. A reporter from The Westen Morning News once described the venue at Par Moor as the 'Wembley of the West.'

Former British Trials Champion Gordon Jackson recalled his friendship with Hussey. Gordon said: 'Gerald or Gerry, as everyone knew him, rode in trials before he became a famous speedway name. He rode at West Ham, where I went to watch him race. He was good, breathtaking in fact. We had a drink together after the meeting. Jackson concluded: 'I was so saddened to hear of his tragic death in a car racing accident in Australia.' Today, Gordon still enjoys watching motorcycle sport and participating in car trials, with some success.

Fred Paul, who lives at Sheviock, near Torpoint recalled that first meeting. He said, 'I had just come out of the Royal Air Force, my wife and I rode down on our B.S.A. motorcycle to watch the racing. We were surprised at the huge crowd. It was five years since I saw any racing at Par Moor. Gerry Hussey and Jack Young seemed to stick in my mind; all in all we enjoyed our evening.' Today Fred Paul is still as enthusiastic about his beloved speedway and will be found amongst the crowd at Plymouth's St.Boniface Arena.

Mike Tremayne, a former committee member of the Pendennis Motorcycle and Light Car Club has fond memories of the re-birth of Cornish speedway. He said: 'My Dad was a farmer and in those days the milking of the cows was done by hand, which took much longer than it does today. We knew we were running close to the start time of 7.45 p.m. and our Austin Ten didn't do the speed of modern cars. When we got there it was a packed house, but they flung open the gates and said "In you go" and Dad never paid!

The stock car event on Tuesday 5 August was hit by bad weather. A crowd of 2,400 people endured torrential rain, which made the track slippery. Following on from that the speedway meeting scheduled for Wednesday 6 August against Poole Pirates was postponed due to the bad weather, which disappointed many fans. Incidentally tourism was growing in the Duchy.

On Sunday 10 August, the East Cornwall Motorcycle Club held a grass-track meeting at Port Looe Barton, West Looe. The fog hit the event hard, but that didn't deter Lew Coffin from Sherborne, who won the 350cc open and dirt-track classes.

St.Dennis rider Adrian Kessell twice finished as runner-up. Interestingly, the St. Austell junior rider Chris Julian was the second fastest rider of the day. Kessell by this time had quit riding on the shale and was winning across the country in grass-tracks. Meanwhile, Coffin, a successful grass-tracker on the continent, did ride for Weymouth Royals but never appeared at the Cornish Stadium.

Chris Julian busy working on his machine.

Regrettably, the next speedway meeting versus Oxford, which was scheduled for 13 August also fell foul to inclement weather, meaning two successive postponements for Trevor Redmond.

Some remember Mr.Redmond for trying to make a shilling, but there was much more to the man than this. Indeed, T.R. had many good points, which must not be overlooked. For instance, he was always the first to carry a stretcher if someone was hurt. Trevor also introduced the opportunity for the spectators to win premium bonds on lucky programme numbers, which was new for its time. Redmond surprisingly fed the schoolchildren too, by distributing 400 free Cornish pasties to the little ones. It was funny talking to people about Redmond. What came across was that he was always true to his word, as I can testify when he supported the riders' reunion at the White Gold Classic and Custom Bike Show, which I organised with a small group of friends in the summer of 1994. Jerry looks at T.R. the showman in the last chapter.

The 1958 St.Austell line-up had a different, cosmopolitan feel to it. Among the riders were Aussie Jack Geran, Kiwi Trevor Redmond, Southampton's Brian Crutcher, Brian Brett and Alf Hagon, South African Trevor Blokdyk, and a youngster who looked to have bucket loads of potential, namely Fraddon's Chris Julian.

Twenty-one year old stock car racer Johnny Marquand of Notter Bridge made the news during August for all the wrong reasons. He allegedly cut a corner, was fined £25 and disqualified for six months for driving without due care and attention. Incidentally, Marquand went on to become a top driver around the ovals of the U.K.

On Wednesday 20 August, St. Austell played hosts to Poole and leading the home side was Ove Fundin. The Swede, who was the 1956 World Champion, rallied his team to an eight-point win over the Pirates. Unfortunately, the meeting was hit by bad weather and was abandoned after heat ten. Returning to the St. Austell team were former Gulls Bob Duckworth and Dennis Newton. Both Chris Julian and Newton overslid on the very tricky surface, with the latter unable to continue in the meeting as a result. Trevor Redmond returned to the saddle, recording a win and a third place finish, before blowing his engine. There is a connection between Ove Fundin and T.R. When Ove got married in 1956 he travelled to Australia with Ronnie Moore and T.R. Being roomed together because of 'the prim and proper rules of the period' Ove obviously became firm friends with T.R.

Ove rode for Trevor on several occasions and did so again when he resurrected speedway at Wembley's Empire Stadium. In an interview with the journalist John Chaplin for his biography Ove recalled how T.R. took him to South Africa. The short race tour usually took in three meetings in a week but it turned out to be a bit of a farce. At one meeting Trevor was riding with Ove but was also referee and timekeeper too. Funnily enough T.R. broke the track record on that evening! Full match result of August 20th: St. Austell 34 points, Poole 26 points. The scorers were St.Austell 34 (Ove Fundin 9; Bob Duckworth 7; Ian Williams 6; Neil Street 6; Redmond 4; Francis Cann 2) Poole 26 (Les McGillivray 7; Birger Forsberg 5; Gerald Hussey 4; Ken Adams 4; Jack Unstead 4; Terry Small 1; Brian Brett 1). The ever-likeable Francis Cann's appearance for the home side started a long association with the club. At this time the official match programme's were selling at just a shilling (5p), they remained at this price throughout the season.

Local lad Chris Julian idolised the Swedish World champion Ove Fundin. It was 'funny' looking back because each became controversial figures, in their own way. Ove had such a talent and passion for speedway he didn't like losing races. If he did he would get so mad with himself. To have ten World rostrum places in consecutive years and four European titles was indeed remarkable. Chris, like his idol some years later, had to be chaperoned from a meeting, being spirited away hidden in the back of the car. Ove's success was not just his consistent riding but the back up he received from his mechanic Les Mullins.

Mullins, who the author met at Hoveton in Norfolk some years ago, was more than just Ove Fundin's mechanic. He did almost everything! Les Mullins also prepared the bikes for the Norwich team for sixteen years. It is good to report the former five times World Champion is again on speaking terms with his talented 'old spanner man'. On 30th.October 2006 Ove was made an honorary freeman of the City of Norwich. During his riding career he became the pride of Norfolk aboard the famous Norwich No.2 track spare. Many veteran riders turned out to support Ove on his special day including world champion Freddie Williams, Trevor Hedge, Len Read, Phil Clarke, Billy Bales and Tich Read. Norwich Speedway historian Mike Kemp was on hand to take notes and photos of this unique occasion. Fundin's biographer John Chaplin flew in from Spain to support him. It became a family occasion with Fundin's son Niklas and grandson's Karl and Gustav being in attendance. Councillor Roy Blower described Ove as 'our greatest sportsman'. The author added, "That said it all for the people of Norwich."

Many still travelled to watch speedway on the train arriving at Par Station. The Great Western steam train 'The Cornish Riviera Express' was often seen pounding by Par Moor and appropriately passing close to the Cornish Riveria Club (later known as the Cornwall Coliseum). Billows of smoke would be seen from Carlyon Bay Golf course to Hillside arch. By the time League speedway had finished the last of the steam trains had ceased and been replaced by diesel locomotives. Suprisingly enough several people still walked to the stadium from outlying areas, from places such as Tregrehan Mills, Bodelva, St.Blazey Gate, Holmbush, Church Road Charlestown and Par Lane.

Wednesday 27 August saw another individual event, entitled the West of England Open. Riding on the night were homester's Trevor Redmond, Francis Cann, Chris Blewett, Chris Julian, and Jack Geran, plus Neil Street, Mike Broadbank, Alby Golden, Trevor Blokdyk, Alf Hagon, Johnny Hole, Ronnie Genz, Ian Williams, Brian Brett, and Gerry Jackson. Unfortunately Maurie Mattingly, Josef Hofmiester, Dick Bradley and Brian Crutcher were not available to ride. Unluckily, Golden fell in heat one and Redruth's Chris Blewett had to lay down his machine to avoid the prostrate rider. The re-run turned out to be a cracker between Street and Broadbank, with the lead changing hands several times as the riders rode wheel-to-wheel. It was Neil Street who crossed the line first, but only by the narrowest of margin's as he established a new track record of 67.8 seconds. Hagon defeated Geran in heat two and also bettered Street's record time, further lowering it to 67.4 seconds. Geran, who then rode for Leicester, had a brilliant meeting and was unbeaten throughout the rest of the night.

Heat eleven witnessed Hagon and Jackson clash on track, with the former eventually winning comfortably with yet another new track record of 67.2 seconds.

Both Street and Hagon finished level on points, with the Aussie awarded second place by virtue of defeating the Englishman when they had met. Full result: Geran 14; Street 13; Hagon 13; Broadbank 12; Jackson 11; Williams 10; Blokdyk 10; Golden 7; Hole 7; Redmond 6; Brett 5; Julian 3; Cann 3; Blewett 0. The race meeting was won by the Australian rider Jack Geran who finally settled in Exeter, buying a house and being adopted by Devon folk as their own. Jack Geran clearly recalls being presented with a cheque for £3,000 by promoter Trevor Redmond. In 1958, this sum of money was like winning the modern day 'lotto', but Geran's luck was short-lived because it was a bogus cheque carefully signed in the name of the Southampton promoter Charles Knott. Redmond was notorious for wrapping trophies and giving special gifts, which usually ended up being an empty box, more of his antics later. Today, Jack Geran lives on the coast at Dawlish Warren.

Former St.Austell Gull Eric Martyn, the Cornwall Centre A.C.U. President who now resides at St Stephen, recalled watching 'junior rider' Francis Cann. He said, "Francis always made a scoring contribution in an easy old style, he was so good to watch. It was a big blow to hear of his passing in 2005, I spent many happy hours in Francis' company, he will be missed by everyone who knew him."

The stock car fans were disappointed with the announcement that another rain-off put paid to their Tuesday night's entertainment. In fact, a decision was made to discontinue the racing for the rest of the year, as the evening light was fading and the days were becoming shorter.

Les Nicholas, a life long motorcycle enthusiast who now resides at Goon-havern fondly remembers his trips to speedway as a youngster. He said,"My Dad was a shift worker at the gas works in Truro, at that time we were living at Chacewater. I think I saw my first meeting when I was nine, which was the 1953 season. In those days it took us one hour and ten minutes to reach Par Moor in Dad's Austin 10, driving into Truro, and through the villages. I even remember the registration number of the car, which was AAF 376. My Uncle Sid Matthews often travelled with us to speedway. I remember the later era better because I witnessed the start of the careers of both Chris Blewett and Chris Julian." Les also recalled watching Bill Uren and Phil Williams going for it in local sidecar grass-track events.

In 1962 like a few young men of that time Les ran off to Gretna Green 'to tie the knot' with his sweetheart Valerie. Sadly paying the rent came before watching speedway at Par Moor. Years later Les Nicholas followed the sport again watching the speedway career of Mike Semmonds of Rejerrah because of his friendship with 'his colourful Dad' Bruce.

Arguably one of the most exciting meeting's of the season was the International Best Pairs and Champion of Champions meeting held on Wednesday 3 September. Despite a poor summer, the riders really entertained the spectators. Over 4,000 people came through the turnstiles despite the fact that Ove Fundin and Jack Young were unable to participate for different reasons. The Aussies paired together were Jack Geran and Peter Moore, while the Kiwi pairing were Ronnie Moore and Trevor Redmond. The All Blacks duo riding were Barry Briggs and Bob Duckworth, with the British Lions being represented by Ken McKinlay and Peter Craven. For Europe, Josef Hofmeister and Dick Bradley were paired together. Finally for the Kangaroos were the duo of Chum Taylor and Neil Street. In a dramatic heat one, Geran seized his engine and Hofmeister wrecked his bike in a bad spill. Local lad Chris Julian kindly stepped in to lend Hofmeister his machine so he could continue in the meeting.

The Lions pair of Craven and McKinlay took the honours on the night with a joint tally of twenty five points. The local newspapers described the diminutive Craven of Belle Vue as being 'in fantastic form.' Despite Briggs' interval apology to the fans for not riding too well, the New Zealander certainly didn't humiliate himself. Barry Briggs and Bob Duckworth were runners-up with seventeen points. In fact, Briggs proved he had all the makings of winning the World Championship again. He went on to triumph in the Champion of Champions semi-final in the second half racing.

McKinlay was second and Ronnie Moore was third. However, it was the diminutive Craven who took victory ahead of Briggs in the final. One week later, under the famous Wembley twin towers 'Briggo' raced to his second world title. Full result of (International Best Pairs): Craven (13.5) and McKinlay (11.5) = 25; Briggs (10) and Duckworth (7) = 17; Street (12) and Taylor (2) = 14; Geran (9) and Peter Moore (5) = 14; Ronnie Moore (7) and Redmond (4) = 11; Bradley (9) and Hofmeister (0) = 9; (Champion of Champions Final): 1st Craven; 2nd Briggs; 3rd McKinlay; (Consolation Race): 1st Duckworth; 2nd Street; 3rd Redmond.

It is worth mentioning that bigger things were on the horizon for Ronnie Moore. 1959 was indeed to be Ronnie Moore's year. No one could stop the Wimbledon captain in the World Final at Wembley. In front of 70,000 fans, he scorched to a 15-point maximum. Moore received speedway racing's most prestigious trophy from John Surtees, who was the World Road-Racing Champion. Best of the 'Brits' was Brian Crutcher who took fifth place. He also appeared in several meetings at St.Austell during the season. Away from the track, Brian Crutcher ran Sea View Car Sales at Parkstone in Dorset.

The final meeting of the season was held on Wednesday 10 September, when the home side took on the Swindon Robins in front of over 3,500 spectators. Drafted into St.Austell's side were Brian Brett, Trevor Blokdyk, Alf Hagon,

CORNISH STADIUM
ST. AUSTELL

WEDNESDAY, 3rd SEPTEMBER, 1958
AT 8 P.M.

International Pairs Contest
and Champion of Champions

Official Souvenir Programme 1/-.

W. & T. Sanders, Printers, St Austell.

Left and above: 3rd.September 1958 Programme cover.

Brian Crutcher and Chris Julian.

Meanwhile, returning to the team was the 'nippy' Australian, Jack Geran riding against a full-strength Swindon outfit. Geran went on to top score for the home club, but they still went down 54-42 to the Robins. Incidentally, Jerry says he pronounces Jack's name, 'Jerran'. England international Crutcher won his first two races then faded badly. Swindon's top performer on the night was Mike Broadbank, who had been a leading qualifier in the World Championship preliminaries. Broadbank was given a standing ovation in heat fourteen when he laid down his machine to save Hagon from serious injury. Hagon had lost control of his machine and swerved across the path of the very fast Broadbank. Although 'Broady' fell heavily, he still went on to win the re-run in his distinctive red leathers. He also produced some fine lads from his successful training school at Rye House. In those days, he used to charge his pupils £1-7-6 per session, a fee that was inclusive of insurance. Fortunately, grass-track expert Hagon wasn't seriously injured. The teams were evenly matched for much of the meeting and after heat ten they were tied on thirty points each. However, three 5-1's from the visitors were to put the meeting beyond doubt.

The completed score chart read as follows: (St. Austell) Jack Geran 17, Brian Crutcher 10, Trevor Blokdyk 6, Trevor Redmond 5, Brian Brett 4, Alf Hagon 3, Chris Julian 0; (Swindon) Mike Broadbank 13, Neil Street 12, George White 12, Dick Bradley 11, Ian Williams 6, Roy Taylor 2, and Maurice Conway 1.

Trevor Redmond remembered clearly he helped feed many of the speedway lads like Brian Brett and Colin Pratt with Cornish pasties before they became household names. Brian Brett who started early on at St.Austell went on to become a good rider for Southampton and Swindon Robins. In 1965 he achieved a sixth place in the World Final at Wembley, scoring a credible nine points. In 1967 Brian moved from the Newcastle Diamonds side to Cradley Heath to be reunited with Cornishman, Chris Julian. Sadly Brian passed away in 2006. His death from a heart attack was a shock to all in the shale sport. Although 'Bretty' retired from the track at a young age and took the final chequered flag much too soon, no one will ever forget his wonderful smile.

Track pusher Robin Hendry said he felt having guest riders such as Barry Briggs and Ove Fundin make appearances at the Stadium helped to swell the crowds. He said, "Lots of people had heard of these star names and they were curious to see how good they really were."

Behind the scenes there were several youngsters keen to have a go. Ivor Toms and Lewis Philp, who had ridden cycle speedway, were soon practicing their broadsiding technique at the Cornish Stadium car park on borrowed machinery. Geoff Kimber who was keen to get into the sport proved helpful by lending Ivor his bike to hone up his skills. Geoff was the wrong build for speedway but it didn't stop him deep down wanting to be a rider until the day fate was to deal him a poor hand. Geoff's machine went up in flames. The wannabe's pooled their money to buy some decent machinery from Jackson's of London. A Rotrax J.A.P. performed better than anticipated and the boy's were set to follow their speedway dream.

Ivor Toms served an apprenticeship with The White Hart Garage in St. Austell, where he drove all his colleagues mad about speedway. He was never available to work overtime on Tuesday nights, which of course was speedway night!

"Incidentally Baron Gray who did much of Trevor Redmond's accounts and secretarial work was a great uncle to a young lad named Roger Whitehouse. Baron regularly used to send St.Austell Speedway race programmes to Roger's family in Birmingham. Today Roger lives in British Columbia and still has his cherished speedway programmes."

1959
The top-flight riders return

C ar racing continued at Par Moor, but unfortunately speedway throughout Great Britain was in the doldrums, with only nine teams operating in
the league. However, Trevor Redmond, who was still enjoying his riding,
continued to promote Open Meetings at the Cornish Stadium with Bob Netcott. The former Wembley star also ran five meetings at Pennycross Stadium,
Plymouth, the first of which took place on Good Friday. T.R. used his connections, pulling in riders Split Waterman, Ray Cresp, Jack Unstead and Harry
Bastable to participate.

This was the age of 'Teddy boys', cinema and television, although many folk
in the Duchy just chose watching speedway to help alleviate their mundane
routine. "It was their style of Edwardian dress which earned them name Teddy
Boys,"said Dave Bartram, the lead singer of fifties revival group Showaddywaddy. "No Ted would be seen without his bright suit with velvet collar, drainpipe
trousers and crepe soled shoes." Today Showaddywaddy are still gigging after
thirty years, they have played in Cornwall several times including at the Cornwall Coliseum (Carlyon Bay), and Hall for Cornwall (Truro). So Rock'n'Roll is
certainly alive west of the Tamar river. Also in this year 'The Mini' designed by
Alec Issigonis was first manufactured in Britain. These small cars were delivered
locally by 'By-Pass Transport'. In later years the cars were raced extensively at
Par Moor

Incidentally World Motor Racing Champion Mike Hawthorn paid a visit to the Par Moor circuit whilst holidaying on the Cornish Riviera during
the summer. Hawthorn, who just edged out Stirling Moss to lift the Formula
One title was captivated by the area and commented how much he enjoyed
'lovely Cornwall'.

The first speedway meeting of the season on 1 July was an individual challenge for the Stars of the West Trophy, which was won by the former Gull, Peter
Moore. During an entertaining evening, Ray Cresp broke the track record,

thereby setting the tone for the season. Cresp had signed for Poole and took over as their number one. Star rider Jack Biggs failed to make match fitness.

On 8 July the Combined Stars met the Swedish Tourists in a grand challenge match at Par Moor. It was a real thriller and eventually resulted in a draw. The Swedes were particularly grateful to Ove Fundin and Rune Sormander, both of whom rode through the meeting unbeaten. Full result: Combined Stars 48 (Geoff Mardon 11; Ken McKinlay 10; Jack Geran 10; Jack Biggs 6; Ray Cresp 5; Neil Street 5; Francis Cann 1) Swedish Tourists 48 (Fundin 15; Sormander 15; Bjorn Knutsson 7; Goran Norlen 4; Kjell Warrenius 4; Bengt Brannefors 2; Hasse Hallberg 1).

A week later on 15 July, a Best Pairs event was held and turned out to be a real triumph for Swindon, with their riders occupying the two top spots on the podium. Full result: George White (11) and Ian Williams (10) = 21; Neil Street (13) and Mike Broadbank (8) = 21; Ron How (12) and Bob Andrews (7) = 19; Peter Craven (10) and Jimmy Squibb (2) = 12; Gordon McGregor (8) and Francis Cann (0) = 8; Jack Unstead (7) and Trevor Blokdyk (1) = 8.

On Wednesday 22 July, a three-team tournament was staged featuring St. Austell, Exeter and Bristol. The home team, who had to fight for every point won by a small margin of just two points.

The result of the meeting being St. Austell 26 points, Exeter 24 points, and Bristol 22 points. The meeting ended with a spectacular crash. During a handicap race, Johnny Hole of Bristol fell heavily and while his machine somersaulted, Aussie international Neil Street crashed into him. Luckily Street walked away unscathed, but the unfortunate Hole was carried off on a stretcher with a back injury. Thankfully though, after first aid treatment from the medical staff, Hole was allowed to go home.

The following Wednesday saw an unofficial challenge match between Ken McKinlay's Lions and Ronnie Moore's Kiwis, which pulled in the largest crowd of the season. Using a cracked frame George White somehow managed to record two heat wins. Meanwhile, McKinlay top scored with 13 points as he captained the home side to victory by 46 points to 44 points.

The next speedway at Cornish Stadium on 5 August saw an unofficial challenge between St. Austell and a team of London-based riders. The Wednesday night racing featured some exciting tussles between first string or heat leaders from both teams. St. Austell only managed to register three heat wins as the Londoners raced to a resounding 56-34 victory. Stars of the meeting were the brilliant Ronnie Moore and Danish ace Arne Pander, who rode for Oxford. Pander was only appearing at Par Moor for his second time, but he made riding the dry surface look so easy. He also gave a brilliant exhibition of team riding with former St. Austell teamster Cyril Maidment. Home captain Jack Geran led by example and was his side's top scorer.

Following the main event, Neil Street took victory in the Carlyon Big Four race beating off strong challenges from Moore and Pander. The completed scorechart read as follows: (St. Austell 34) Jack Geran 11, Ian Williams 9, Neil Street 8, Jimmy Squibb 3, Trevor Redmond 3, Chris Julian 0; (London 56) Arne Pander 15, Ronnie Moore 14, Cyril Maidment 11, Nick Nicholls 10, Graham Warren 4, Johnny Board 2.

The following Wednesday (12 August) came a three-way challenge between a British Lions squad, a Continental Select and a Kangaroo's Select. The Lions were led by the 'pocket rocket' Peter Craven. It was touch and go whether the meeting would be held at all because the previous thirty-six hours had seen five-and-a-half inches of rain. Between 10-13 August the area saw 'torrential rain and flash flooding'. St. Blazey and Par experienced the worst of the weather, which caused devastation to homes and families. In particular, Station Road in St Blazey was hit very hard, with many cottages being swamped by the floods, as the ground floor furniture, fixtures and fittings, were ruined by the smelly deluge of water. In fact, a lot of folk remember these events to this day.

Amos Putt of St.Blazey a keen speedway enthusiast throughout the years, picked up the story, stating, "Villagers worked hard to fill sandbags to keep the water back. The canal was the highest I had ever seen it. Down by Brooks Corner the flood-water was deeper and people were being ferried to safety by rowing boats and punts.' He concluded: 'Speedway was a big part of my young life. I have fond memories of Par Moor and saw it right through to it's closure at the end of 1963. The Gulls never had a home advantage because the well-prepared track rode equally well for the visiting teams." Today, Amos a local councillor is well known for his charity work.

Not wanting to disappoint the fans, Trevor Redmond pushed ahead with the meeting on 12 August and he was rewarded with a surprisingly large crowd. The action proved to be entertaining with Bjorn Knutsson providing some thrill-a-minute riding. Meanwhile, Alby Golden set a few hearts a fluttering in heat three when he missed the gate, but came through from last to first in impressive style. The Continentals were without the injured Ove Fundin, so Chum Taylor deputized despite being from Down Under. Even Peter Craven was beaten in his first two outings on the night. The leading performer for the Continentals was Swindon star Tadeusz Teodorowicz. In conversation, future Gull Glyn Chandler described the Polish rider as 'classy'. The Continentals amassed 35 points, winning nine of the twelve heats. Peter Craven, the 1955 World Champion, scored ten points and led the British Lions to second place with 23 points. The surprise of the meeting was the eclipse of the Kangaroos who only collected 14 points, with their solitary heat win supplied by Neil Street. Full result: Continentals 35 (Teodorowicz 10; Knutsson 9; Birger Forsberg 8; Taylor 8); British Lions 23 (Craven 10; Ian Williams 6; George White 4; Golden 3); Kangaroos 14 (Jack Geran 5; Ray Cresp 5; Street 4; Aub Lawson 0). Second-half activity saw Forsberg win the All-Stars Scratch event from Knutsson, while both Ivor Toms and Chris Julian appeared in the junior racing.

On 19 August, the next track action was the Cornish Best Pairs contest, which saw Jack Geran and Neil Street gel together brilliantly to triumph after bagging twenty one points. The winning duo subsequently collected their awards from Edith Netcott. Behind the victorious pair, Ken McKinlay and Maury Mattingly tallied 19 points, while also finishing on the same total were Arne Pander and Nick Nicholls. Looking further down the scorechart, Graham Warren and Ron Mountford totalled 14 points, while Francis Cann and Ian Williams had 11, with Chris Julian and Ivor Toms bringing up the rear on 6. Incidentally, the victorious Street sported the colours of Plymouth Devils on the night! Also held on a busy evening was individual fare for the 50 Guineas Trophy, which had been donated by Bob aka Colonel Harry Llewellyn.

Many folk remember the meeting as Toms' coming of age; after all, he had started as complete novice at the beginning of the season, but revealed great potential by taking a second place and two thirds in the event. The trophy also presented by Mrs.Edith Netcott, went the way of McKinlay, who won all of his heats to collect a fifteen-point maximum. He was a tad fortunate in heat eight however, when Mountford's engine died whilst he was leading, gifting the Scotsman the win. Full result: McKinlay 15; Geran 13; Pander 12; Williams 10; Mountford 8; Street 8, Warren 7; Mattingly 4; Toms 4; Board 2; Julian 2, Cann 1; Philp 1. There was some consolation for Chris Julian late in the evening, when he won the Cornish Handicap race. Julian was one of Cornwall's promising riders.

Margaret Bird of Park Way, St.Austell has fond childhood memories of her nights at speedway. Her Mum and Dad, Eileen and Ron Bassett were keen supporters. Ron who was a track pusher travelled to the stadium on his motorcycle or scooter whilst Margaret and her Mum went on the bus. Eileen and young Margaret regularly met up with Mickey Luxon's wife and watched the racing at the track with her. Mickey who was a colleague of Ron at John Williams Joinery was also a 'pusher'.

Margaret chuckled as she said, 'I was only about eight or nine years old when I started attending speedway. Dad made us and many other fans too, plywood boards with 'a crocodile clip' to hold our programmes.'

She concluded, 'No fancy programme holders from a shop in those days. Mum and Dad loved speedway so much they went to many World Finals at Wembley. During the interval I enjoyed the packet of crisps with the blue salt bag, then it was just a few heats before the journey back by bus. We met the bus at the Britannia Inn and the driver dropped us off at Bethel Chapel.' Margaret's Dad, Ron Bassett continued helping in speedway when the sport was revived in Cornwall in the nineties. In 2001 Ron was captured in a rare video interview with presenter Brendan Joyce. When introducing Pit Marshall Ron to the viewers Brendan explained how Brent Werner was probably the first American star to ride in Cornwall for fifty years. The first was the great Wilbur Lamoreux, who was one of the top five riders in the world during that postwar period. Ron had seen 'Lammy' ride at Par Moor and other stars like him even at Rocky Park prior to that. Brendan gave Ron a duplicate copy of the match programme for his scrapbook, which Bassett very much appreciated. Ron said, "Speedway is a friendly sport, I have many great friends through the track including names like Neil Street and Jack Geran." When asked the million-dollar question did he prefer the racing of the old days or the modern 'Premier League' Ron had no hesitation in his reply, he said, "The Premier League racing here has been exceptional, it has been a great joy to watch, I miss it every winter."

On 30 August a letter was sent to the editor of the Cornish Guardian newspaper, complaining about the noise of the public address system at the speedway on Wednesday evenings. The resident of Sunny Cottage, Carlyon Bay was incensed by what he described as an 'an inferno of noise.' He finished his letter by explaining that for over 30 years he had lived within a stones throw of the Empire Stadium, Wembley, which, during that time, had never subjected local residents to an infernal row. It is worth noting that some forty-five years later, certain individuals still moan incessantly about noise levels despite motorcycles and stadiums adhering to stringent regulations. In 2005 as the future promoter was putting his proposals together a small lobby of residents undoubtedly put pressure on Restormel Borough Council who opposed the track being rebuilt further along Par Moor.

The penultimate meeting of the season took place on 26 August and it was a cracker, with something for everyone. The main event was a three-team tournament involving St. Austell, Poole and Wimbledon, but there were other ingredients including the new craze of go-karting, which was demonstrated by Ronnie Moore, Gillian Carlyon and Trevor Redmond. The attendance, estimated to be in excess of 3,500 were treated to some exceptional racing, including a dead-heat between Ken McKinlay and Moore. Had the 'Scottish Express' got the edge over the Wimbledon international he would have posted a deserved maximum, only just missing out by half-a-point. Also appearing was another special guest rider for the home side, none other than Nigel Boocock, who missed a place in the World Final by just 1-point. The three-team tournament was hailed as a great success almost as soon as McKinlay had equalled the track record of 66.6 secs in his first ride of the evening.

The home side went on to win thanks to the injection of some on form guests. Moore and McKinlay rode wheel-to-wheel in one heat, with the Scot just having the edge. Full result: St. Austell 32.5 (Ken McKinlay 11.5; Neil Street 9; Nigel Boocock 6; Jack Geran 6); Wimbledon 27.5 (Ronnie Moore 10.5; Cyril Maidment 8; Bob Andrews 7; Cyril Brine 2); Poole 12 (Jack Biggs 6; Ray Cresp 3; Birger Forsberg 2; Trevor Blokdyk 1).

In the Nations Cup, Moore took the honours, being followed home by Boocock and McKinlay. Meanwhile, Ivor Toms won the sidecar event ahead of Roy Wedlake.

It was still possible to see one of the local boys from St Blazey Gate or Holmbush climbing a tree to watch the speedway, although not in the numbers which had been seen a decade before. In the 'pioneer years' the boys in the trees appeared like starlings! Sometimes, workers from Heavy Transport yard were also seen on top of the fuel tanks trying to get 'a bird's eye view' during their meal breaks.

The final meeting of the season was run on Wednesday 2 September at 7-45 p.m., when an Overseas All Stars side, captained by Barry Briggs, took on Ken McKinlay's British Lions Select. McKinlay's team included Ian Williams, Ron Mountford, Cyril Maidment and Mike Broadbank. Briggo's side included

Graham Warren, Ronnie Moore, Neil Street and Jack Geran. Local junior riders Chris Julian, Francis Cann, Ivor Toms and Lewis Philp all took part and they said they thoroughly enjoyed the experience. Lew Philp won the Junior Racing on that evening. The match resulted in a 40-32 success for the Overseas All Stars. Two speedway sidecar demonstrations were put together by drivers Roy Wedlake, Ivor Toms and Chris Julian.

Ken McKinlay's track record of 66 3/5 seconds held firm for another year. The evening was sprinkled with Sports car racing. There were three heats of racing with two going into the Sports Car Trophy Final.

The season was deemed a success having given the public a chance to see plenty of quality riders including the calibre of Barry Briggs, Ronnie Moore, Peter Moore, Cyril Maidment, Jack Biggs, Ray Cresp and Birger Forsberg to name but a few. Michael Rowe of Rosehill, St Blazey, a keen supporter at this time, thought the riding of Briggs was sensational and that he really stood out from the crowd. Today, Barry is officially retired but is still involved in the sport. The celebrated commentator and journalist Dave Lanning once said: 'Frank Sinatra did it "My Way", Briggo did it the 'Hard Way.' The author agrees with that entirely, Barry deserves every bit of credit for his contribution to two-wheeled sport, including his MBE. Jerry said, "I met Mr. Barry Briggs at the Speedway/Grasstrack Show at Coventry a few years ago and found him to be such a joy to talk to. Barry who was 73 years old at the end of December, still spends part of his year in the U.K.

Reg Fearman the former Test rider for England in the fifties spoke to me briefly about his friendship with Trevor Redmond. He laughed, "Many remember the comment aimed at T.R. from some bright spark when he joked, he'll never squeeze into his leathers." Reg was also a successful team manager and promoter at Middlesborough and Halifax but is remembered for riding for the famous 'West Ham Hammers'. During the sixties Reg formed a business partnership with Mike Parker but prior to that he was rightfully praised for helping to launch the Provincial League in 1960. Reg was a person who used the centre-green microphone to great advantage.

He was a promoter who exploited interval attractions and chatting to guest stars from the world of television, which was still increasing in popularity. The author recalls how big the 'Bush' television set in his home appeared to him as a small boy and being fascinated with a new channel called BBC 2.

Trevor Redmond set up a 'Pirate' meeting at Cradley Heath in 1959, which aroused a lot of interest. Following this event a meeting was called in Manchester. The new Provincial League was formed under Auto Cycle Union rules.

Reg concluded, "I always kept in touch with Trevor, and from time to time our paths would cross. I was delighted to attend Trevor Redmond's seventieth birthday celebration, but was very saddened to learn of his passing only a few weeks afterwards. He is still missed!" Today Reg lives in Provence, France. He is still very active and organised a wonderful 80th birthday celebration for former St.Austell Gull, Jackie Gates. Reg and Eileen Fearman co-ordinated the event with Goldcoaster Bluey Scott for forty of Jack's best mate's and a sprinkling of speedway royalty to be at Jack's surprise party. Race legend Ivan Mauger was there, so was Arthur Payne, Allan Quinn and John Titman.

Winding back the years Mrs.Muriel Mason of Camelford fondly remembers the night's they watched speedway at Par Moor 'before they married'. She said, "My future husband 'Gerald' and I used to attend the race meeting's regularly in the late fifties.We met many lovely friend's through speedway including Mr.and Mrs.Arthur Squires and their daughter Barbara, plus the Hocking family of St.Blazey. Today Gerald still has a keen interest in speedway and enjoys riding his B.S.A. motorcycles."

1960
Using promising local talent

Many of the young speedway fans were off to the 'big school'. Penrice-School on Charlestown Road opened it's doors for the first time in January 1960. Today the school is known as Penrice Community College and boasts new Art and I.T. facilities. Also in this year St.Austell Garden Centre just a few hundred yards from the stadium opened it's gates for the first time. The horticultural establishment has changed proprietors over the years and been known as 'Veermans' and 'Prices'. Sadly their entrance has been a notorious 'accident black-spot' over the year's which has included motorcycle fatalities.

Meanwhile the St.Austell Gulls now appeared to have their own shape and form by using the local talent. The established riders were Chris Julian and Ivor Toms, while other local lads were Stratton's Ray Wickett and Chris Blewett of Redruth, who supplied the thrills whenever he rode. Among other regulars were George Major, Exeter's Francis Cann, former Oxford and Cardiff rider Frank Johnson, and of course we must not forget dear old T.R. who despite having the nickname 'Fats' could still reel in the silverware when on song. In those days, Charlie Lobb acted as team manager but we know T.R. was the real organiser.

George Major speaking to me from his home in the Isle of Wight, said, "First of all I did cycle speedway which I enjoyed, then I became acquainted with T.R. I first met Trevor Redmond in 1960 when I was riding with my first club Aldershot."

Trevor, of course had been a top man at Aldershot in the fifties before they closed down, which was a big attraction for us. I was fairly new to the game and just had to pass everyone, which I could do going into a bend when I slowed a bit, but usually ended up whacking the fencing on the way out. That's how I rode around Aldershot, bouncing off the fence all the way for four laps, or sometimes less! This day was no exception, I could keep passing Trevor going in, but he could easily pass me coming out while I was in No Mans Land. He must

Chris Julian and Chris Blewett in action, photo L.J.Heaman, St.Austell.

have been impressed though, as he asked me if I would like to ride at St.Austell in open meetings during the summer."

George continued, "I accepted his offer and travelled down from Oxford with veteran rider, Frank Johnson. What a character he was, but that's another story. Trevor was absolutely amazing at Par Moor, he did just about everything. He would help prepare the track and introduce the riders on parade. On occasions he would operate the turnstile, or help direct operations in the car park. Then he came rushing into the pits at the last minute, warm up his bike, go out and win a race, run on to the centre green to lead the fans on the microphone in a war-cry 'Up the Gulls' and run back for his next ride."

Ray Wickett, early on in the season had a few rides at Bristol, from these outings he made two life-long friends in Cliff Cox and Chris Julian. He was actually signed by Suffolk club Ipswich, but didn't get a first team place so they loaned him to Plymouth for two years. Over the next three seasons, Wickett was in and out of the St. Austell team. The author said, "I recall him saying he was coached and encouraged a lot in the early days by Mike Broadbank, who was influential in getting him started in the sport. In his latter years, he rang me quite often and I always endeavoured to keep him in touch with his old pals."

It was during this period that local workers rode to work in the thriving clay industry on motorcycles such as a B.S.A. Bantam, Triumph Tiger Cub, Greeves, Francis Barnett, Ariel Leader, James Captain and Velocette Vogue. It wouldn't be long though before Alan Damerell of Whitemoor would be selling Japanese step through motorcycles, the world was changing! Today Damerell's are set to move to new premises at Indian Queens, just off the main A30 trunk road which will include ultra modern workshop facilities.

John Milton recalled to the author at a motorcycle meeting how one of the gang of local bikers pitched a British Cotton machine against a new 100cc.Suzuki in a run off up Pentewan Hill. The buzzy heal and toe change Suzuki easily outperformed the Cotton. The British bike stalled half way up and protested noisily on restarting. Despite this the J.A.P. engine was still winning on the speedway track though. The name, J.A. Prestwich was one of the most prolific engine manufacturers of all time.

On Tuesday 12 July, Trevor Redmond and Chris Julian won a 'Best Pairs' meeting at Par Moor. Redmond had to been seen in action to be believed.

Trevor sold programmes to the punters as they came in, then announced the teams on the centre-green before changing into his black leathers. He proceeded to ride his socks off! When he wasn't riding for the Gulls, he was riding for his parent club Bristol. In the Bulldogs' colours, later that year he won the Provincial League Riders' Championship at Cradley Heath with a fifteen-point maximum. Ken Middleditch and Eric Hockaday finished next in that order. Redmond had a memorable year where he topped the scorers at St. Austell, with seventy-five points from a short season.

Despite poor weather in the opening 'Pairs Competition', a crowd of 2,500 enjoyed the speedway, which was blended with some car racing. Cliff Cox and Johnny Hole who represented Bristol, scored a combined total of 14 points to finish as runners-up. Redmond would have had a maximum from his rides if he hadn't coaxed his partner home in the final heat. Toms was unlucky in his third race, when he broke a chain. Full result: St. Austell 'A' 19 (Redmond 11; Julian 8); Bristol 14 (Hole 7; Cox 7); St. Austell 'B' 11 (Francis Cann 8; Ivor Toms 3); Poole 10 (Geoff Mudge 7; Charlie Wallis 3) Cradley Heath 6 (Ronnie Rolfe 6; Vic White 0).Following the race meeting there was speculation whether St. Austell might also sign Aussie Johnny Board and Bengt Brannefors, the Swedish rider. Incidentally, adult admission prices to the stadium for the meeting were 3/6 (17.5p) or 5/- (25p), while children were charged 1/6 (7.5p) or 2/- (10p).

Francis Cann grabs a drink while working on his bike, photo L.J.Heaman.

The season saw an upturn in the fortunes of the sport with the formation of the new Provincial League, which boasted ten teams. T.R. just wanted to be part of that!

Speedway had been staged at all ten venues before, but no matter, at long last the sport was moving forward instead of being in the doldrums. St.Austell still operated as a non-league side with an open licence, but the new league meant more teams could race against the Cornish Gulls in competitive matches.

On Tuesday 19 July, St.Austell met a Rayleigh side in an eleven-heat challenge with five riders in each team. To be fair it was more of a Rayleigh Select since they had to borrow Swindon's Johnny Board to complete their side.

The Australian showed just what an excellent choice of guest he was by topping the Rockets' scorechart with eleven well taken points. Both the local and speedway press commented on the standard of racing, describing it as 'great' and it was clear that the spectators had enjoyed a value for money meeting. The Gulls came out on top too, winning by a 6-point margin and they owed much to their skipper Trevor Redmond, who returned a wonderful full five-ride maximum. As if riding and promoting at Par Moor wasn't enough for him, Redmond was also riding for Bristol Bulldogs in the Provincial League,

Chris Julian leads the pack, photo Eric Martyn.

as indeed were his teammates Chris Julian and Ivor Toms! Chris was seen in several second half events and Western Cup matches. Full result: St. Austell 36 (Redmond 15; Julian 11; Francis Cann 5; George Major 4; Toms 1) Rayleigh 30 (Board 11; Eric Hockaday 8; Stan Stevens 6; Ken Vale 3; Reg Nicholls 2).

A week later, on Tuesday 26 July St. Austell took on Cradley Heath in another challenge fixture. The highlights of the night's action were the tussles between visiting star Colin Gooddy and St. Austell skipper Trevor Redmond. The two met four times, but Redmond only beat his rival once! In the Scratch race Gooddy beat Redmond by only the width of a tyre. It was good to see the remarkable improvements of St. Austell's young riders. Francis Cann and Ivor Toms finished as equal top scorers with 11 points apiece. Full result: St. Austell 45 (Toms 11; Cann 11, Redmond 10; Julian 10; George Major 2; Ray Wickett 1); Cradley Heath 27 (Gooddy 14; Ronnie Rolfe 5; Tony Eadon 4; Roy Spencer 2; Steve Collins 2; Vic White 0). In the second half scratch races, there were wins for Collins (heat one), Major (heat two) and Gooddy (heat three).

Turning to the sidecars, heat one was won by Eric Roberts from Alan Humphries and Roger Eddy, while heat two resulted in victory for Phil Williams, who was hotly pursued by Roy Wedlake. Finally, in the handicap event,

A rare shot of Roy Wedlake (with cigarette) chatting to former Gulls rider and manager George Newton. George. a Pre-war track star, was the chief pit steward at Par Moor and went on to coach for the Plymouth Devils in 1969.

Williams took the chequered flag from Eddy, with Humphries in third spot. Prior to the next meeting, the hot news during the week was that St. Austell completed the signing of former Belle Vue, Cardiff and Oxford rider Frank Johnson.

The racing on Tuesday 2 August saw two of the most spectacular crashes ever seen at the Par Moor track. The Gulls played host to a Commonwealth Stars Select, captained by former St. Austell rider Bryce Subritzky. The first crash involved novice rider Ray Wickett in the second half. He lost control of his machine and the bike double somersaulted before coming to rest. Luckily, Wickett was able to get up and walk away. The other crash involved Padstow's sidecar crew of Alan Humphries and Jim Crews, who flipped their outfit in virtually the same spot on the track. The outfit was badly damaged breaking into pieces as it came back to earth, but thankfully neither driver or passenger, were badly injured. The result of the meeting was a narrow defeat, with the Commonwealth Stars edging victory by 34 points to 32.

The scores were: (St. Austell) Trevor Redmond 10; George Major 6; Frank Johnson 5; Ivor Toms 5; Francis Cann 3; Chris Julian 3; (Commonwealth Stars) Subritzky 10; Johnny Board 9; Geoff Mudge 8; Gerry Bridson 5; Eric Howe 2; David Dodd 0. Following the main event, Chris Blewett won the reserves' race, while Poole's Geoff Mudge won the Par Scratch Race.

Johnny Board took the 'Big Four' contest from Redmond, which was run from a rolling start. In the sidecars Roy Wedlake of Carclaze had a good night, first tasting victory in heat one. Eric Roberts won heat two, but it was Wedlake who triumphed in the final. Each time out the diminutive Phil Williams was sandwiched between Wedlake and third man Pat Crawford of Saltash.

As a point of interest, the methanol for the speedway machines was carried week by week to the Cornish Stadium by Trevor Kessell, the younger brother of the veteran motorcycle ace Adrian, who still participates in grass-track racing to this day. The younger Kessell was quite happy to undertake this duty and still managed to do it when he broke his leg. In this month Trevor's brother Adrian, and the former Gull and St.Austell rider Francis Cann won their finals in the Broadhembury Club Grass-track.

'Kes' was riding well in grass-tracks away from Cornwall, but often found he had to take a minor rostrum place behind Lew Coffin.

On Tuesday 9 August the St. Austell team played host to Poole in a Western Challenge Cup meeting. The day had been hot and humid leaving the track very dry so Trevor Redmond and his staff decided it desperately needed watering. They watered for a couple of hours, then at 7.00 p.m. as the spectators were entering the stadium, the sky simply emptied. The match went ahead, however, and it was a credit to the young St. Austell side that they won the meeting by a seven-point margin. Chris Julian and George Major both suffered falls, but picked themselves up to ride again. The team-work and bonding was really beginning to show. Full result: St. Austell Gulls 39 points, Poole Pirates 32 points. St.Austell 39(Colin Gooddy 8; Redmond 7; Francis Cann 7, Julian 6; Ivor Toms 6; Frank Johnson 5; Major 0); Poole 32 (Tony Lewis 12; Ross Gilbertson 7; Norman Strachan 7; Geoff Mudge 4; Jim Gleed 2; Allan Kidd 0; Charlie Wallis 0). In the second half, Jim Gleed took victory in the reserves' race, while Roy Wedlake won both sidecar heats.

Bristol Bulldogs visited Par Moor Stadium for a second Western Cup meeting on 16 August. An exciting meeting ensued and the result was in doubt until the final chequered flag, finally ending in a draw. Chris Julian was excluded for 'boring' in heat three, but he still went well to bag six points for the home side. The highest scorer for Bristol was Pat Flanagan with nine points. In the second half of the programme, Chris Blewett and George Major claimed a win apiece from the two reserve races, while the sidecar spoils were shared between the local crews of Phil Williams and Roy Wedlake. Full result: St. Austell 36 (Redmond 12; Julian 6; Francis Cann 6; Ivor Toms 5; Major 4;

A great portrait shot of
Chris Blewett of Redruth, photo
Eric Martyn.

Frank Johnson 3) Bristol 36 (Pat Flanagan 9; Johnny Hole 8; Cliff Cox 7; Ernie
Baker 6; Frank Evans 4; Eric Howe 2).

Moving on another week to Tuesday 23 August the home side beat a powerful team of young stars from the Midlands. The weather was kinder and it was
a great night, with the result again depending solely on the last heat.

Tension was mounting as the riders went to the tapes. After a false start St.
Austell's young riders did their stuff, with George Major and Chris Blewett taking a deserved 5-1.

St.Austell's aces gave their side a narrow success. It had been an exciting match
for the local fans as in heat nine Trevor Redmond fought off the challenge of
Harry Bastable and Johnny Board to take the win. Again in the second half,
Roy Wedlake dominated the sidecar events. The match result was St.Austell 38,
The Midlands Stars 34. The full results, St.Austell (Redmond 11; Francis Cann
9; Major 5; Chris Blewett 5; Chris Julian 5; Ivor Toms 3); Midland Stars 34
(Bob Jones 9; Harry Bastable 8; John Board 8; John Hart 5; Ronnie Rolfe 3;
Eric Howe 1).

On 26 August the Cornish club travelled to Knowle Stadium to participate
in a Four-Team Tournament. The homesters, the Bulldogs were the victors se-

curing 31 points, St.Austell were second with 24 points, Yarmouth were third with 22 points, and finally Poole brought up the rearguard with 19 points.

Brian Annear talked to the author about his memories of helping Trevor Redmond. Brian became close to T.R. and saw many things behind the scenes which many spectator's would not have been aware of. Brian has done a lot for Cornish motorcycle sport, from being a well-known figure with his spares van at Moto X meetings to being the inspirational promoter to resurrect speedway at Claycountry Moto-Parc in 1997.

Brian said, "Trevor once bought a job lot of tankards for prizes but they didn't have any bottoms. So he cut out cardboard bottoms and still gave them out as trophies. His regular bit of nonsense with trophies was that he always asked for the trophy to be returned for engraving. One week it was for pairs, another for an individual meeting, then it became the 'All Star Trophy'. He was always up to something but you couldn't but like him."

The meetings at Par Moor came thick and fast, with the home side only suffering defeat on one occasion against Bryce Subritzky's 'Stars' line-up on 2 August, when they went down by just 2 points. On Tuesday 30 August in a three-team Tournament, the Gulls' riders rode for the 'West' side. The North won the meeting with 26 points, while the South and West teams finished as joint runners-up on 23 points each. Riding in the meeting was Jack Kitchen, who was the nephew of the Cornish Stadium track designer Bill Kitchen, a man who had been associated with Duchy track racing since the 1930s. Jack Kitchen's 12-point tally certainly helped the North to their victory over the South and West sides. In his second ride Kitchen met Trevor Redmond who pushed him so hard, his time was only 0.8 of a second outside the track record. Between them, Kitchen and Stoke's Ken Adams scored 22 of the North's 26 points. Incidentally, it was Adams who went ice racing on the continent with Cornishman Bruce Semmonds in the early fifties. St.Austell were the West representatives but were frankly a wee bit under strength.

Ivor Toms only took one outing because he was still suffering the after effects of a nasty fall at Bristol. In the second half, there were some spectacular crashes, with a particularly memorable one involving 'the thrill a minute rider' Chris Blewett of Redruth, who wrecked his machine in the process.

The full result: North 26 (Kitchen 12; Adams 10; Jack Winstanley 3; Bob Jones 1); South 23 (Gerry Bridson 8; Ross Gilbertson 7; Norman Strachan 6; Jimmy Gleed 2); West 23 (Redmond 10; Chris Julian 7; Francis Cann 4; Toms

A more sombre reflective Chris Julian, photo Ron Bassett.

1; Blewett 1). Despite his crash, Blewett went on to win the reserves' race, while Kitchen beat Adams in the Par Scratch Race final. Although Roy Wedlake won the sidecar heat, it was Pat Crawford who took the handicap race.

The final home match of the season was scheduled for 6 September against Bristol, but it was rained off. Keeping faith with the public, the clash subsequently took place the following week on 13 September with the usual 7.45 p.m. start. It was a needle match because a month earlier the two teams had ridden to a 36-36 draw at Par Moor. Aside from that the Gulls had lost by a narrow margin at Bristol, going down 38-34 on 2 September. Complications arose in that both Trevor Redmond and Ivor Toms also rode in the colours of Bristol at Knowle Stadium! However, Redmond proved to be in unstoppable form as he bagged 12 points for the homesters. Although Bristol put on a plucky performance, they still ended up losing. The main disappointment for the visitors was Cliff Cox, who was usually a good scorer at the Cornish Stadium, but only notched 2 points on this occasion.

Full result: St. Austell 40 (Redmond 12; Toms 10; Chris Julian 9; Francis Cann 7; George Major 2; Chris Blewett 0; Ray Wickett 0); Bristol 31 (Johnny Hole 10; Jimmy Gleed 8; Cyril Francis 5; Frank Evans 3; Ernie Baker 3; Cox

2). In the second half racing, Eric Howe was first past the chequered flag in the reserves' race. Howe was closely followed over the finish line by local riders Ray Wickett and Eric Roberts. Meanwhile, Francis Cann won the Par Scratch Race which topped off a good season. Ivor Toms won the Cornish Championship with Wickett finishing as runner-up. Fittingly, Redmond won the Big Four Event, which was the finale to a great evening's racing.

Author Jeremy Jackson asked Ivor Toms about his connections with former World Champion Tommy Price. He explained that Tommy did his engines for him in the early years and later he was blessed with a wonderful friend in Fred Hicks of Redruth.

Hicks always helped maintain the machine belonging to his brother Telfer who rode on the local grass-tracks and also appeared in second half racing at the Cornish Stadium. Toms, who travelled up and down to Redruth commented: 'Fred often helped out.' Fred and Mary Hicks are probably better known as founder members of the Cornish Solo Grass-track Club. Fred and Mary's daughter Brenda Quintrell supported by her husband Mark have followed in their footsteps by giving many thousand's of hours of service to Cornish Grass-track. Their son Jake also enjoys participating.

Away from home, the Gulls rode in another two matches - one at Bristol and another at Exeter. In a four-team tournament at Bristol they were runners-up to the home side. The other competitors in that meeting were Yarmouth and Poole. Late in the season, they took part in a Western Cup encounter with Exeter at the County Ground. The home side dominated early on and looked stronger in depth as they swept to a convincing 45-27 success. St. Austell's Chris Blewett who always provided plenty of thrills, was a casualty on the night, being taken to hospital with concussion following a collision with the steel safety fence. Sadly Chris had many breaks in his career.

As an unknown quantity to his opponents, Blewett was unpredictable and often tried to squeeze through gaps that sometimes weren't there! Malcolm Simmons has described Chris Blewett as 'a nutter' in his biography which has infuriated the author who met Chris at his home before his untimely passing. Jeremy said he thinks Chris was courageous, plucky and determined which is a more accurate description the former Gull.

The season proved to a successful one with good local support. Trevor Redmond topped the home scorers with a total of 75 points. He was followed by Chris Julian (48), Francis Cann (45), Ivor Toms (31), George Major (21),

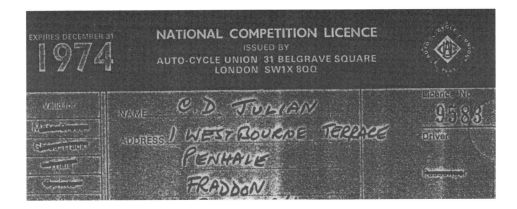

Copy of Chris' competition licence.

Frank Johnson (13) and Chris Blewett (7). The three best sidecar crews were Roy Wedlake, Phil Williams and Pat Crawford.

This was the start of an exciting career for the jovial Chris Julian, who was a hard man on the track and many a time swapped punches in the pits with other riders, including on occasion his own teammates! Charlie Knott signed him to ride for the Bulldogs and he stayed with them until Knowle was sold. What came across to me in the short years I knew Chris was he always lived life on the edge, but whatever he did, he gave his best. People gave him respect because in the dedication stakes he always gave 100 per cent. He could notch tyres, build engines, weld a cracked frame and ride in such spectacular style. Journalist and author Jeff Clew recalled Julian blasting around the County Ground some years later at break neck speed only wearing his ordinary clothes - no helmet, leathers or boots! The late Chris Julian once said: "Thee never knows what'll 'appen when we be racing." Clew commented: "In my opinion he could have gone so much further than he did in speedway because he was an individual rider and not a team man."

Reg Bazely had his memories of the Cornish Stadium. Reg, who was a Foxhole lad by origin worked in the White Hart Garage in St. Austell and was also Eric Perryman's brother-in-law. He said: 'Eric Perryman and Chris Julian were stable mates in Cornish grass-track circles and represented the county in the Cornish Inter Centre Team under manager Bill Adams.' Reg also said he worked for a short period with a young Ivor Toms, who used to attend Cornwall Technical College at Camborne riding a Panther motorcycle. Reg concluded: 'There were many pranks executed in the garage trade back then, some we are unable to safely repeat within the confines of this book.'

Adam Faith and the Roulettes came to City Hall in Truro during the season taking part in a charity raffle. The prize was a Lambretta scooter, registration number 1 UAF, a Cornish number but also the pop star's initials. Jack Collins of 'W.H.Collins of Truro' shook hands with the singer who went on to be a star of stage and screen. In television he had a few successful series' such as Budgie and Love Hurts. The singer appeared as a guest at several London Speedway Stadiums but sadly not at Par Moor.

Malcolm Ball of St. Austell reminisced about his friendship with Ivor Toms and the late Lewis Philp. When Ivor was riding for St. Austell, he let the young Malcolm try his bike around the track at Par Moor. He said: 'It gave me a feel what it was like to ride a speedway bike but I never opened it up!' During this period Toms and Philp formed a partnership and ran a garage off Stannary Road, Stenalees. Malcolm said: 'I was lucky because I watched speedway at the Cornish Stadium on Tuesdays and then travelled to Pennycross Stadium in Plymouth with Ivor and Lew on Wednesday evenings.' Both lads rode at Plymouth when they held open meetings. After a while the pair moved their car venture to Trezaise Road, Roche.

Malcolm concluded: 'During this period we were fortunate to see so many good riders - Peter Craven, Barry Briggs and Ken McKinlay to name just a few.'

With the season over and Christmas approaching, the granite building in the town adjoining the White Hart Hotel which housed the town library was demolished. It would be years before the new building was ready. Today St.Austell awaits a large injection of funding and rebuilding of the town-centre. With hindsight many mistakes were made by the St.Austell Chamber of Commerce in the sixties.

1961
A varied programme

The destruction of the old St. Austell town began in this year. The buildings in what would become Trinity Street went under the bulldozer. The Baptist Church was spared and still stands in the twenty-first century. Within the space of a year a new road would be created to link Truro Road and Bodmin Road with South Street. In January 1961 the St. Austell Urban District Council asked the County Planning Authority to earmark Rocky Park for possible use as a heliport. Rocky Park had been used both for landing planes and motorcycling events before the war. The site, only a mile from the town centre opened up all sorts of possibilities for Cornish people. Sadly it never materialised. "In January 1961 it was announced in the Bristol Evening Post that Knowle Stadium was to close. Local speedway riders Chris Julian and Ivor Toms both spoke of their happy times at the stadium on Wells Road. They concluded Knowle should not have been sold." On a dull February morning in 'sixty one' Trevor Redmond attended the first speedway reunion at High Beech. It was a day for signing autographs, mixing with the old riders and walking what was left of the old track. Today, each February, speedway's roots are remembered with a similar gathering and a collector's fayre on that spot.

In this year Chubby Checker inspired the new 'twist' dance craze which was seen at a few of the supporters club events, aided I'm told by various beverages purchased from the bar.

H.R.H. Prince Philip paid a visit to St. Austell on 6 May, being flown in by helicopter. He visited St. Austell Grammar School (now Poltair Community College) and the clay works. Needless to say, the 'Royals' never witnessed any track action at Par Moor. It is strange though if it was a football or speedway at Wembley there was usually some representation of Her Majesty. "It has been suggested in much of the speedway press H.R.H. Prince Philip hasn't watched a speedway match since 1948."

Grass-track racing was the only motorcycle action to grab many enthusiasts until the shale action started. In June, at the Pendennis Motor Cycle Club arena grass-track at the Royal Cornwall Showground, scrambler Brian Slee took the 500cc honours. The runner-up was Adrian Kessell of St Dennis and third place went to St. Just rider David Harvey.

"Former South Cornwall Speedway Club official Bill Martin of Redruth spoke to the author many years ago about how the Tourist Trophy races became part of their year. He said, "We used to go over whenever we could. In June 1961 Mike Hailwood became the first rider to win three T.T. races in a week. People just didn't believe it. Over the years Hailwood became a T.T. legend taking fourteen Island wins." Colin Martin said "Dad went racing somewhere every weekend when I was in my youth." When Colin was 16 he rode a DOT in scrambling against his Dad. Bill in his retirement gave pleasure to hundreds of people demonstrating a Dirt Track Douglas around the old vehicle rallies and festivals of Devon and Cornwall. Bill passed away in October 1996 but was indeed a character and is sadly missed."

Robin Hendry one of the track pushers has fond memories of Par Moor and wanted to record a few of the things he saw from the pits. Robin explained, "Many of the pushers T.R. used were employees of John Williams Joinery including myself, on our way home from work we went straight to the stadium to water the track. Sometimes it needed doing, on other occasions it started raining before the meeting commenced. Most of us at that time rode motorcycles, Geoff Jarvis had a Triumph 21, Ron Bassett a B.S.A. C11 and Frank Bazeley a B.S.A. Bantam. Frank, a work colleague who helped us in the pits each week broke the kickstart off his bike, so he had to bump start it. In the pit area there was a dump area for old oils and that sort of thing. Frank started to bump off the Bantam, when it overslid on the oily patch and over he went. Ron Bassett and Geoff Jarvis were in hysterics. Needless to say Frank never lived it down when he returned to work." Robin concluded, "I also recall on occasions the meetings were held up briefly because we had to wait for the medical officer Dr.Houston to be in place. Also the rivalry between the neighbouring clubs of Exeter and St. Austell often boiled over into throwing of blows and insults. Chris Julian was one who could hold his ground on and off track! Finally in my opinion I enjoyed watching the sidecar boys race, I got to know many of the local drivers like Phil Williams and Ken Westaway. What they did took a lot of courage."

On 1st.July a baby girl by the name of Diana Frances Spencer was born in

Norfolk. Who could have guessed this girl would have such an impact on the twentieth century by marrying the Duke of Cornwall! As far as speedway was concerned the season kicked off on 4 July with a pairs event for the Stars and Stripes Trophy. The Poole duo of Geoff Mudge and Allan Kidd won the meeting. The short season continued with open meetings at Par Moor with many of the St. Austell riders doubling up, riding at Plymouth and Exeter.

The following week (11 July) in their first team event of the year, St. Austell crushed Wolverhampton in a challenge encounter. The flicker of gossip around the terraces was about the 'new kid in town', namely Wayne Briggs. The sixteen-year-old was only known to most folk as the younger brother of former World Champion Barry Briggs, but he showed the home crowd he had talent by scoring a maximum. Indeed, Brigg's brother gelled particularly well with Francis Cann of Exeter as the pair took 5-1s from all their ride's together. St. Austell had an able guest rider in the shape of Poole's Geoff Mudge, who bagged eleven points for the home side. Likeable Aussie Graham Warren skippered the Wolverhampton team, but didn't show any of his normal blistering form after taking 'a heavy tumble' in heat one.

Full result: St. Austell 48 (Briggs 12; Mudge 11; Chris Julian 9; Cann 8; Chris Blewett 4; Ray Wickett 4; Reg Hawken 0); Wolverhampton 29 (Vic Ridgeon 10; Warren 5; Eric Eadon 5; Eric Howe 3; Cyril Francis 3; Bob Warner 2; Bill McGregor 1). It was Mudge who won the Big Four event in the second half, while Bill McGregor won the reserves' race. Phil Williams took the main sidecar event and Edward Kent won the Sidecar Handicap race. In the Wednesday evening grass-track at Newquay, former St. Austell rider Adrian Kessell was in winning form taking victory in seven out of eight races.

Tuesday 18 July saw St. Austell beat a local side, which provided stiff opposition. Roy Bowers captained a challenge select known as the Devon Devils. Bower's team was made up of Provincial League riders from Plymouth and Exeter. Years later, a Devon Demons side was to ride at Exeter's County Ground.

It was a hero's return for promoter Trevor Redmond, who had been out of action since the previous autumn following a serious racing accident in Sweden. The Kiwi stepped in to take the place of Chris Blewett, who had suffered a bad crash the previous Friday evening at Wolverhampton. Although T.R. displayed flashes of his old form, the top scorer for the St. Austell Gulls was Geoff Mudge. For the opposition Maurie Mattingly rode well, sharing top spot on the score-chart with Cliff Cox on eleven points apiece. Full result: St. Austell 42 (Geoff

Mudge 10; Chris Julian 8; Redmond 8, Martin Ashby 6; Francis Cann 6; Ray Wickett 3; Reg Hawken 1); Devon Devils 36 (Maurie Mattingly 11; Cliff Cox 11; Norman Strachan 4; Eric Howe 4; Allan Kidd 2; Terry Stone 2; Howdy Byford 2).

Incidentally, Poole's Allan Kidd was seen promoting cigarettes in speedway magazines and journals at the time, as well as on television, something that would be a taboo practice today of course. He was seen building models, viewed as a family man but also pictured at break neck speed going into a bend 'without brakes'. The second half racing proved entertaining as ever. In what was billed as the Roaring Reserves' Race, Eric Howe won through from local lads Eric Roberts and Reg Hawken.

In the Four Stars heat it was Norman Strachan who took victory, with youngster Martin Ashby on his tail in second place and Terry Stone in third spot. In the Big Four it was Bristolian Cliff Cox who took the spoils. The Sidecar heats were a little more shared around than normal. Vic Skinner took heat one from Phil Williams. In heat two Edward Kent won from Alan Rowe and Eric Roberts, while the Handicap race resulted in another success for Kent.

It is important to note the new Tamar road-bridge opened, making the local derbies so much easier to attend. Ray Sparks, a Plymouthian and former mechanic to Alan Smith commented that getting down to Cornwall for an evening match was never easy. The queue on the Plymouth side for the Torpoint Ferry started by mid-afternoon. He said: 'On the way back from a meeting at Par Moor we were often queued back into the town of Torpoint waiting what seemed to be an eternity; we had many late nights!' So the bridge solved the traffic congestion, but gone were the banter and signing of autographs by the waiting riders as in years gone by. Who would think forty years later they would add two more lanes of traffic, with the author and Plymouth colleague David Irvine inspecting the temporary gantries for lifting in sections to carry the new centre roadway.

George Major explained how his season started, "In 1961 I signed a contract with my home town club, Oxford who were a first division side. They promptly put me on loan to Newcastle. Their race night being Monday meant I could not ride St. Austell open meetings on Tuesdays, in any case I crashed out with a broken jaw for eight weeks, so my racing was pretty limited that year."

On Tuesday 25 July speedway fans witnessed the rise of future England star Martin Ashby, who at only seventeen years of age won the Cornish

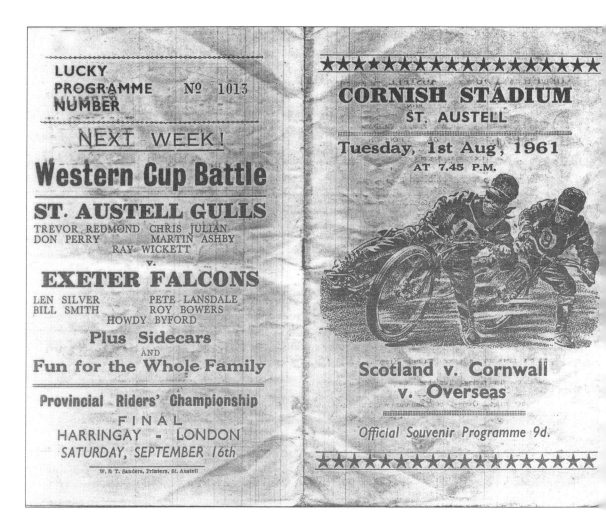

Programme cover 1st August 1961

Championship at the Cornish Stadium. It was a good evening for the youngster from Great Bedwyn, near Marlborough. He missed a maximum by just two points against some high calibre riders, three of whom rode in Swindon's National League side. The event came to a dramatic climax after the junior rider had tied on points with Provincial League Riders' Champion Trevor Redmond. It was ironic that T.R. would have to ride off against Ashby because he had brought the Wiltshire boy to Cornwall for the first time in 1960. At Bristol Martin Ashby soon developed the nickname 'Crash' because he certainly cut his speedway teeth at their track, with several falls along the way.

Redmond and co-promoter Bob Netcott saw talent in the youngster and T.R. would have to call on all his valuable experience in an effort to deny him in the run-off. Ashby had won the inside gate and as they lined up at the tape there were a lot of girls cheering for him. The tapes went up and he made the gate. T.R. did everything he knew to pass over the four laps, but Ashby hung on, to the sound of tumultuous applause from the crowd.

Unfortunately, in the pairs contest that followed, Ashby's running mate Wayne Briggs (the younger brother of Barry) had an off night and they could only register 17 points between them as victory went the way of Geoff Mudge and Brian Brett. Meanwhile, Redmond and Brian Meredith finished as runners-up. One could speculate that had Meredith got his machine started for his last heat they may have actually won the meeting.

Regrettably though, he was excluded for missing the two-minute time limit. The author recalls meeting Brian Meredith at the Speedway and Grass-track Show at Coventry. Jerry said Brian Meredith was obviously delighted to reminisce about the old days with my friend and travelling companion Ivor Toms. Full result: (Cornish Championship) Ashby 13; Redmond 13; Mudge 12; Brett 10; Chris Julian 7; Maury Mattingly 6; Bob Roger 6; Bob Jones 6; Meredith 6; Francis Cann 5; Briggs 4; Ray Wickett 2; Eric Roberts 0; (Best Pairs result) Mudge and Brett 22; Redmond and Meredith 19; Ashby and Briggs 17; Julian and Cann 12; Roger and Jones 12; Mattingly and Wickett 8. I noted Eric Roberts deputised twice for Maurie Mattingly.

In a Three-Team Tournament on Tuesday 1 August two seventeen-year-old junior riders went through the card unbeaten from their first three rides. Wayne Briggs went on to complete a full maximum for the 'Overseas' team, while Martin Ashby's winning streak was cut short in the final heat. Their wonderful performances made the headlines in the following week's local press, thus: 'Teenagers thrill crowd with fine riding.' One of the other side's was a 'Scotland' team, for whom Bill McMillan rode instead of George Hunter. Heat one saw Redmond post a win over Scotland's Jimmy Tannock, with Francis Cann filling third position to give 'Cornwall' a good start.

It was a treat for the fans to see the veteran Dom Perry back in speedway. Perry had given up the sport in 1956 while at the top and spent five years concentrating on his farm near Dublin. Joining Perry were Globe of Death rider Dick Campbell and fellow New Zealander Alf Wells. Ashby and Chris

Julian added another five points for Cornwall in heat two, before repeating the dose in heats four and nine. Meanwhile, Briggs followed Ashby's lead along with his teammate Perry as they rode to 5-1s in heats five, seven and twelve. The meeting was a close run thing and the last heat would decide whether the Overseas' team or Cornwall would take the spoils. The final heat saw Julian, Ashby, Perry and Briggs go up to the tapes. It was a thrilling climax with the two youngsters coming head-to-head for the first time on the night. Ashby made a poor start and it was Briggs who pulled away to win in the fastest time of the night, 70.8 seconds.

Meanwhile, in the battle for the minor scoring positions, Perry held off Ashby's challenge to give the 'Overseas' side victory. Full result: Overseas 29 (Wayne Briggs 12; Dick Campbell 7; Perry 6; Alf Wells 4); Cornwall 27 (Ashby 10; Trevor Redmond 7; Chris Julian 6; Francis Cann 4); Scotland 16 (Doug Templeton 7, Willie Templeton 7; Jimmy Tannock 1; Bill McMillan 1)

In the second half racing, the Reserves race' was won by Alan Mann of Edinburgh who defeated local lad's Reg Hawken and Eric Roberts. While in the Stars' Scratch event it resulted in victory for Ashby, ahead of Cann and Alf Wells, 'The Par Scurry' went the way of Briggs from Julian and Templeton, while the United Nations Scratch race saw Perry take the win ahead of Redmond and Campell. Completing a busy programme, it was Pat Crawford's night in the sidecar events as he won the first Scratch race by a good margin from Roy Wedlake with Eric Roberts in third place. Then, in the Handicap race both Wedlake and Crawford started 40 yards back, but it was Crawford who fought his way to the front for another excellent win. Edward Kent brought up the rear of the field.

The next meeting on 8 August was a Western Cup battle between St. Austell Gulls and the Exeter Falcons, who were captained by Pete Lansdale. It proved an entertaining scrap with its share of thrills and spills. The first races were shared, prior to the Gulls recording successive 5-1s to the cheers of the home crowd. After Heat Seven St. Austell had built up a ten-point advantage, but unfortunately it didn't last. Following a bad tumble in heat eight, Exeter rider Frank Johnson was taken off on a stretcher. Johnson sustained bruising to his knee and ankle, so didn't take any further part in the evening's racing. Exeter clawed their way back into the meeting and with two races remaining they only trailed by four points. However, the Gulls held on to win in the end, their final margin of victory being six points. Stan Stevens top scored with nine points for the home side, but it was a good team performance from the St. Austell lads who really fought for every point. In contrast, Lansdale netted 13 points from five rides for the visitors, while Howdy Byford's contribution was 9 points, also from five starts. Full result: St. Austell 42 (Stevens 9; Trevor Redmond 8; Francis Cann 7; Chris Julian 7; Dom Perry 6; Wayne Briggs 4; Alan Mann 1) Exeter 36 (Pete Lansdale 13: Byford 9; Roy Bowers 5; Len Silver 5; Frank Johnson 2; Eric Howe 1; Billy Smith 1).

In the second half racing, Alan Mann won the reserves' race, beating Eric Roberts and Reg Hawken. Other races saw Francis Cann take the Stars' Scratch event, while Dom Perry won the Par Scurry. The Big 4 race saw Trevor Redmond emerge victorious, with Phil Williams winning the Sidecar Scratch race and Pat Crawford tasting success in the Handicap race ahead of Roy Wedlake. Incidentally, Williams was pitched 60 yards back and just couldn't make up the gap. In each sidecar race Alan Rowe was unplaced. A seventeen-year old girl who lived in Birmingham wrote to the St. Austell promoter asking whether she could have a go as a sidecar passenger. The letter was passed to the pits for a reply but we have not established whether her dream was fulfilled.

The match between the Gulls and Exeter reminded author Jeremy Jackson of a story Ron Bassett (one of the St. Austell track staff) had told on a few occasions. Chris Julian and Len Silver had an altercation on returning to the pit area. Swearing ensued followed by blows of fists and Bassett had to wade in to part them. Some thirty years later when Len Silver visited the Claycountry Moto-Parc, pit marshal Ron Bassett reminded him of the story and he chuckled!   A common advertisement in the St. Austell programmes of this era was an offer on the Remington Roll-a-Matic shaver for the princely sum of £9-15-0 (£9-75)

On 15 August St. Austell took on neighbours Plymouth Bulldogs. Jack Scott couldn't ride for Plymouth so Cliff Cox reverted back to his role with the Bulldogs and the Gulls operated the rider replacement facility. With only three races to go it looked like St. Austell had the meeting in the bag. Holding a 21-15 advantage, it meant Plymouth would have to win all three heats to triumph.

Trevor Redmond produced some of his best riding of the season against Cox and Maurie Mattingly of Plymouth, but despite his best efforts, he was unable to prevent Plymouth from sneaking an unlikely victory by a narrow 2-point margin. Full result: St. Austell 26 points, Plymouth 28 points.

The scorer's for St. Austell were (Redmond 13; Francis Cann 7; Julian 6; Eric

CORNISH STADIUM
ST. AUSTELL
Tuesday, 15th Aug., 1961
AT 7.45 P.M.

GULLS v. BULLDOGS
Sidecar Championship Thrills

Official Souvenir Programme 9d.

LUCKY PROGRAMME NUMBER No 0514

NEXT WEEK!

THE MIGHTY

Poole Pirates

INCLUDING

CAPT. ALAN KIDD   GEOFF MUDGE
KEN MIDDLEDITCH   ROSS GILBERTSON
TONY LEWIS   NORMAN STRACHAN

v.

ST. AUSTELL GULLS

TREVOR REDMOND   CHRIS JULIAN
FRANCIS CANN   WAYNE BRIGGS
BOB JONES, ETC.

Another Important

WESTERN CUP MATCH

W. & T. Sanders, Printers, St. Austell

Reg Hawken in the colours of Plymouth, 15 August 1961, photo L.J.Heaman.

Roberts 0) Plymouth 28 (Mattingly 11; Ron Bagley 6; Cox 5; Colin Thomas 4; Reg Hawken 2). I note: before anyone thinks about writing in concerning Plymouth being known as the 'Bulldogs', this is 100 per cent correct and Ray Wickett, Chris Blewett and Chris Julian appeared in several meetings for them!

In the pits Bruce Semmonds who lived at Rejerrah chatted to former team manager George Newton swapping tales of the good old days. Meanwhile Ivor Toms had his leg out of plaster.

In the sidecars, Phil Williams beat Roy Wedlake in heat one. However, in the Cornish Sidecar Championship, Wedlake turned the tables on Williams to take the title. His passenger, Reg Hawken won the reserves' race, while Ron Bagley took the Par Scurry and Trevor Redmond won the Big Four event. The evening was rounded off with something a bit different, namely scrambling. Former Gull Adrian Kessell of St.Dennis won heat one, followed in by West Cornwall's Roger White and Redruth's Melroy Youlton. Victory in heat two went the way of Colin Thomas. The scrambles final was subsequently won by Kessell, ahead of trials expert Colin Dommett from Truro, with White in third spot. Incidentally, Colin Dommett went on to lift ten Cornwall Centre Trials Championships, a First Class Award in the I.S.D.T., representing Great Britain and clinching the coveted European Sidecar Trials crown with Eric Chamberlain in 1977. Today Dommett who lives at Tiverton in Devon is known as a great motorcycle presenter and commentator.

In conversation with the author Kessell said he had competed against the best of the scrambling world in a few short years including many works riders. Kessell commented: 'We were struggling to compete on equal terms 'with them' on a limited budget.' He continued, 'If there were Championship rounds in the West Country we felt we were only riding to make up the numbers.' Despite his disappointments and obvious frustration it is plain to see the St.Dennis all-rounder was a keen and skilled competitor.

Today, Adrian Kessell aged eighty years of age is still busy in his workshop as well as riding in grass-tracks, sprints and hillclimbs. To call Adrian Kessell 'a Super Veteran' is simply the truth. His racing successes on grass makes him an all time great, being a National Best Pairs winner, Cornwall Centre Champion,

The winner Adrian Kessell pictured here in a local trial, photo J & S Publications

Midlands Centre Champion, South of England Centre Champion and a National Vintage Champion. He has survived setbacks including several broken bones, having a collapse in 1974 when he was advised to retire, and having his precious trophies stolen from his home in 1992. Adrian is part of a family who have been leaving it's mark on motorcycle sport for 80 years. Will 'Kes' be riding as we go into print? It has to be worth a bet!

An interesting discovery came from the programme of this meeting because it gave the names of Eric Abbott and Owen Ward in the Rodeo Overdraft heats. For those who don't know those names, let me explain further. The late Eric Abbott contacted me when he was in such poor health from his sick bed in Pontefract Hospital.

Eric who lived in Plymouth in the old days finally settled in Knottingly, West Yorkshire. He said, 'I bought an ailing J.A.P. from Lewis Philp in 1960. I thought I had died and gone to heaven!' He continued: 'With my friend Owen Ward from Saltash we had several rides at the practice sessions at Par Moor. From this induction Trevor Redmond gave us budding wannabe's rides in the Baby Bubble or Rodeo Overdraft heats.' Eric was fortunate to build a friendship with both Chris Blewett and Chris Julian, who organized things so that Eric could practice on farmland in East Cornwall. Eric Abbott rode in only five meetings before packing it in; financial constraints and a wrecked bike forcing an early retirement. Having got married, his family tried their best to apply pressure on him to quit the shale riding. One week Abbott explained to his friend Jack Summers, that he couldn't ride, so he would lend him the J.A.P. Unfortunately Jack wrecked the bike and hence Abbott never rode again. Despite the misfortune it never stopped him from having a passion for speedway, as he stated humorously: 'I recall the spills too, once I 'whacked' the fence twice in one night, winded myself and broke my teeth!'

On Tuesday 22 August St. Austell met Poole Pirates in a Western Cup encounter. It was an exciting match, in which the home side fought tooth and nail. The Gulls were without Francis Cann, who had fractured his collarbone at Exeter County Ground raceway, the night before. Roy Taylor, who had been filling a reserve berth for the home side wasn't available either. Meanwhile the Poole side were without the talented Ken Middleditch and pinched local lad Reg Hawken as their reserve. The Pirates made a good start, only for St. Austell to pull back again. The Gulls ought to have won several more heats, but were hit by mechanical troubles on several occasions.

With two races to go, the sides were level pegging, but having pulled back 6 points the gremlins again hit the St. Austell lads. In the penultimate heat Chris Julian fell, gifting the Pirates a 4-2. Luckily, he wasn't injured but it meant Trevor Redmond and Brian Brett had to pull back 2 points in the final race of the match. It wasn't to be as Ross Gilbertson rode a blinder of a race to deservedly complete a maximum. Redmond did all he could to catch his opponent, but Gilbertson determinedly held off the challenge. The status quo prevailed and the Gulls lost by 2 points. Full result: St. Austell 38 (Redmond 8; Brett 7; Julian 7; Bob Jones 6; Wayne Briggs 5; Colin Pratt 3; George Summers 2) Poole 40 (Gilbertson 12; Tony Lewis 10; Geoff Mudge 8; Allan Kidd 4; Tim Bungay 4; Norman Strachan 2; Reg Hawken 0.) You will doubtless recall Colin Pratt has since become a successful promoter, at Rye House, Cradley Heath and latterly with Coventry.

In the sidecar racing Pat Crawford took heat one from Alan Rowe and Eric Roberts. In heat two Phil Williams and Roy Wedlake were the only finishers. In the final Williams alias Phil Silvers won again. The visiting riders made a clean sweep of the second half racing; Ross Gilbertson won the Big Four, Geoff Mudge took the All-Stars event and Tim Bungay was victorious in the reserves' race.

On 29 August, the Cornish Stadium hosted an All Star Pairs Meeting for the Capstan Cigarette Trophy. This included cash prizes and cigarettes. The press flyers also scheduled a full programme of second half racing plus two sidecar races. The management enticed people to come along to win free cigarettes, something which would be frowned upon today.

The Plymouth pairing of Cliff Cox and Maurie Mattingly went on to emerge triumphant from the pairs event after defeating Trevor Redmond and Chris Julian in a dramatic title run-off. Brian Brett who was paired with Bob Roger scored eight points from his first three rides then he became involved in an unfortunate mishap. Brian made his way from the pits, stopping the bike and looking down. He must have felt something was wrong but didn't know quite what it was. Brian bounced the bike up and down a bit on the front forks a number of times but still went to the tapes to start. Away they went, as they turned into the first bend Brian's frame broke and he ended up in the fence. The race was stopped and Brian was excluded from the re-run.   He took no further part in the meeting having sustained a heavy fall. Thirty year old Cliff Cox recalled his pre-match nerves in an interview, stating: 'I know what it was

Cliff Cox in action at Par Moor, here leading Colin Thomas. Allott and Turner are at the rear.

like with your stomach turning over; it's an uncomfortable feeling, but one must control it to succeed. The enjoyment in racing is having success and it was nice to win the Capstan Cigarette Trophy with Maurie.' At the conclusion of the meeting a collection was held for the St John Ambulance Brigade, which amounted to £12-11-8 (approximately £12.58). During the research for the book Cliff Cox has also sadly passed away.

The full match result: Mattingly (14) and Cox (5) = 19; Redmond (14) and Julian (5) = 19; Ross Gilbertson (8) and Tim Bungay (7) = 15; Brian Meredith (10) and Wayne Briggs (4) = 14; Brian Brett (8) and Bob Roger (5) = 13; Eric Howe (8) and Bob Innocent (1) = 9.

The final meeting of the season on 5 September was spoiled by rain. The St. Austell side was strengthened by the inclusion of Geoff Mudge and Nick Nicholls as they entertained Ipswich in a challenge fixture. Despite the weather, a large crowd turned out to see the riders perform in atrocious conditions. Emphasizing this, any rider who missed the start soon had his goggles filled in! Chris Julian was on top form and would have scored a maximum if he hadn't overslid his machine in the last heat. Nevertheless, it was Julian's fearless riding that gave the Gulls the edge over the Witches. Full result: St. Austell 27 (Julian 9; Mudge 8; Nicholls 7; Trevor Redmond 3) Ipswich 21 (Jimmy Squibb 10; Les McGillivray 5; Trevor Blokdyk 3; Colin Gooddy 3).

In the second half Reg Hawken won the Reserves' race in impressive style, while Jimmy Squibb took the Witches Which event, before Chris Julian topped

Chris in the pit area at St. Austell
photo R. Bassett.

off a superb evening by winning the Gulls Farewell. St Dennis all-rounder Adrian Kessell won his scrambling heat to qualify for the final, which he subsequently won from runner-up Monty Osborne. The sidecar racing saw Phil Williams take a spectacular spill in his first outing of the evening. Phil spun around on the wet track and then totally capsized, throwing his passenger out in the process. Luckily neither was hurt and typically, Williams had a grin on his face from ear to ear. Williams never appeared fazed by an incident. In the end it was Roy Wedlake and passenger Reg Hawken who won the Carlyon Sidecar Cup. In their final address of the season Trevor Redmond and Bob Netcott promised they would be back in 1962 and thanked everyone for their support week after week.

Trevor Redmond had another successful year on track but had the cruelest of luck in his defence of the Provincial Riders' Championship at Harringay. On the evening in question T.R. rode in the body colours of Wolverhampton. He was leading from the 'Rayleigh Flyer' Reg Reeves when he lost his primary chain whilst turning into the final bend. Reeves took full advantage of his misfortune to take the title. Trevor Redmond had to be satisfied with second place after defeating Plymouth's Maurie Mattingly in a run-off.

Away from the track in the autumn of sixty-one a model was displayed of a heated swimming pool for St. Austell by the local council. It is hard to believe but it took over a decade to become a reality. On 30 November 1974 Polkyth Leisure Centre was opened. It boasted a heated pool, squash courts, trampoline, a large multi function hall, café and bar.

1962
The Neath meetings come
to Cornwall

George Major explained how Trevor Redmond had contacted him in the winter to tell him he was opening a new track at Neath and would he be interested in riding. He said, "I was over the moon, as it wasn't too bad to get to from Oxford. That's where I met Glyn Chandler, Glyn had ridden for Ringwood Turfs, Eastbourne and Swindon Robins before I started riding. He had a short loan period with Exeter. He was only a teenager and was a top prospect but suddenly after a couple of seasons had retired. He came back to ride for Neath, and was a friendly guy. Trevor had lured him away from the grasstrack scene. After only a few meetings, one night I was having a bit of trouble with my van, but managed to hobble home. During the week Glyn phoned my works foreman, no mobile phones back then, to ask how I got on. Ginger had told him I would not get my van fixed in time and would miss Saturday's meeting. Glyn said, tell George I will pick him up. So he drove from Cirencester to Oxford, back past Cirencester, to Neath then after the meeting drove past home to Oxford, then back to Cirencester, which was in excess of one hundred and sixty miles extra."

" I was astounded, I could not believe a speedway rider would do so much for a sprog like me. After that we became firm friends and are still today, though living on different islands means meeting up is a less frequent event. We travelled together, alternating our vehicles for two seasons at Neath and St.Austell." Today Glyn lives in Alderney and George lives in Shanklin on the Isle of Wight. Glyn chuckled when he recalled having to pump the brakes on George's old van.

He said, "One day near Newcastle under Lyme we came over a hump back bridge quite fast, we met a scooter in the middle of the road waiting to turn right. By the grace of God, George got the brakes to work and we

Glyn Chandler in the pits, photo Ron Bassett.

narrowly missed the rider but had everything which wasn't tied down thrown into the front with us. We were knee deep in engine parts, spanners and everything but the kitchen sink." Many great memories for Glyn!

Tuesday evenings were now firmly established as speedway's night again. Trevor Redmond had no worries about making a success of open season racing at Par Moor, but also had his mind firmly set on Neath in Wales. He made a brave attempt to reintroduce the sport in the Principality under the banner of Neath Welsh Dragons. Indeed, Redmond laboured hard on the Abbey Stadium, living on site in a caravan with his wife and young child in the wettest springtime for many years. He amazed many of the pundits by putting together a Welsh side at all. Well, he cheated a little by asking Ian Williams to persuade Glyn Chandler to join him. He also brought in George Major, who was then sporting a goaty beard, plus former Gull Roy Taylor. Together with the up and coming grass-star Jon Erskine, South African newcomer Howdy Cornell and with the shy Australian Charlie Monk, he had a team.

T.R. opened at the venue on 28 April following a rain-off seven days previously. Regrettably, bad weather was to cause a congested fixture list and a lack of floodlighting which in turn led Redmond to ask the Control Board for permission to run some of Neath's meetings in Cornwall, which they granted.

Ultimately poor attendances at Neath meant the Welsh venture was to be short-lived and they didn't run beyond the 1962 season. Probably the greatest success of the project was the discovery of Jon Erskine.

George Major again takes up the story, "Neath didn't go too well for Trevor, with small crowds, which was something to do with the smallpox scare at that time. To cut his losses he switched his League fixtures to St.Austell. Trevor had run the last league meetings at Neath in semi darkness as there was no lighting. The punters used to park their cars on the banking down the back straight and after a race finished all blew their horns, they were the forerunners of air horns! Trevor had this great idea if they could switch their headlights on during the race we could all 'see better'. It was great until the meeting finished and half of them couldn't start as their batteries had gone flat."

George Major enjoyed recalling this story about T.R. "Once he was called before the powers to be, I assume the Speedway Control Board, to explain why he had not run the meeting at Neath on the Saturday. Trevor's excuse was that we had ridden at St.Austell the night before and it was too much to expect the riders to travel up for the next day. They then produced the results of the Edinburgh meeting where Glyn Chandler, Roy Taylor and I had accepted an open booking. We had shared the driving all through the night and the next day to get there, pre-motorway days of course. At the next meeting, Trevor came in the pits wound up like a clock spring, spitting nails he was, to tell us that he'd been fined and us B------s could pay it! Well, we just fell about laughing and after a while he began to see the funny side."

Eric Boocock, the former England manager recalled how in his riding day's the summer holiday traffic caused problems for T.R. as a promoter. The journey to Neath proved to be a nightmare. Middlesborough rode at Plymouth in a Provincial League match, their next meeting being at Neath. Having set off in convoy they carved their way up through Devon to find they had missed the ferry to take them into South Wales. They then incurred an arduous journey into Wales through the mountains to Neath. After a quick non-scheduled toilet stop Eric slipped twenty feet down a steep slope from where he had to be rescued. Meanwhile the lads rang T.R. to say they would be late. Typical T.R. he improvised by running the second half first.

On the 9 June Neath hosted a World Championship qualifying round. Middlesborough's Eric Boothroyd won the meeting, scoring fifteen points. Redmond who was back racing after an injury was second with fourteen points.

Alan Goodman of Rugby, Warwickshire has an affinity with spectators from the Duchy because he has regrets of never going to watch speedway at Abbey Stadium. Due to Neath's remote location and being so short lived many never witnessed 'racing on a shoestring.'

Many track-racing fans tried to juggle watching grass and shale action. During the 1962 season Adrian Kessell of St Dennis and Bideford's Peter Jeffery gave Lew Coffin of Sherborne some very stiff opposition in the South-West Centre. Fraddon's Chris Julian was also carving a name for himself on grass.

This was the era when family cars were vehicles such as Ford Zephyrs or Zodiacs, Morris Minor's or Mini's, Austin A35s, Standard Vanguard's, Vauxhall Cresta's, Hillman Minx's or Triumph Herald's. Today these vehicles will either be seen in museums or polished up for the Steam and Vintage Rallies.

The short season of racing began on 3 July with a pairs meeting for the Inter-Town Trophy. To add a little more interest each of the participating pairs represented a Cornish town. Wayne Briggs and Francis Cann were allotted Liskeard, while George Major and Glyn Chandler were representatives for Bodmin. Geoff Mudge and Chris Blewett were the riders for Redruth. The city of 'Truro' was represented by Tim Bungay, and Jon Erskine. Chris Julian and Ray Wickett represented St. Austell, with Howdy Cornell and Dave Collins given the job of representing the seaside town of Newquay. Briggs and Cann gelled well together and went on to lift the trophy. Indeed, the 18-year-old Briggs carded a full 15 points from his five rides, shrugging off the question about making the long journey from Edinburgh to ride in Cornwall. Runners-up, just a couple of points behind, were Chandler and Major. It was worth noting that Major's riding had improved considerably since he started with the St. Austell club in 1960. Full result: Liskeard 23 (Briggs 15; Cann 8), Bodmin 20 (Major 14; Chandler 6), Redruth 17 (Mudge 12; Blewett 5), Truro 13 (Bungay 9; Erskine 4), St. Austell 9 (Julian 7; Wickett 2); Newquay 8 (Cornell 5; Collins 3).

In the battle for sidecar supremacy, Roy Wedlake and Pat Crawford locked horns as usual. However, mechanical gremlins put paid to the spectacle. In his first race Crawford's chassis broke, leaving Wedlake to win ahead of Phil Williams. In the handicap event Wedlake's clutch cable fractured gifting the win to

Williams, with Alan Rowe coming home in second place.

On 10 July the first Provincial League match took place at Par Moor and saw Neath defeat Edinburgh. Incidentally,the 'Provincial League' was sponsored by the cigarette manufacturers 'Senior Service'. Trevor Redmond was astute because he knew if one of the 'Dragons' was injured he could pull in one of the St.Austell rider's to fill his place. The highlight of the meeting was the tussle between Redmond and the ever-improving Wayne Briggs. Redmond succeeded in showing the keen youngster a clean pair of heels. The match was won in the first six heats as the home side opened up a 24-12 advantage. After that they only won one more heat, but overall they gave a good match display, running out victors by 6 points. Full result: Neath 42 (Charlie Monk 11; George Major 10; Redmond 8; Glyn Chandler 7; Howdy Cornell 2; Jon Erskine 2; Fred Powell 2) Edinburgh 36 (Alf Wells 13; Briggs 9; George Hunter 5; Willie Templeton 5; Dudley McKean 2; Doug Templeton 2; Jimmy Tannock 0). (Incidentally Monk's real christian names were Warren Edric)

In the second half racing Wayne Briggs took the honours, winning the Cornish Sling Trophy. A spectacular crash occurred near the start/finish line in the sidecar racing. One of Cornwall's top sidecar crews was involved in the incident. Roy Wedlake and passenger Reg Hawken battled through to challenge Pat Crawford for the lead in the handicap event, however, on the back straight the two outfits appeared to just touch. Wedlake's machine hurtled into the safety fence and somersaulted over. A clearly shaken Hawken walked to the ambulance, but Wedlake had to be carried off on a stretcher. Both were subsequently taken to hospital. Wedlake sustained chest injuries and was detained, while Hawken was allowed to go home.

Wedlake's condition was given as satisfactory in the press the following morning. David Stephen's who was Phil Williams passenger commented how Wedlake's tubing to the sidecar frame had fractured during the collision.

A week later on 17 July, the Neath/St. Austell team took on a Stoke side captained by Ken Adams in a Provincial League encounter. The newly assembled team easily overcame the Potters, who were joint league leaders going into the match. In netting13 points, Adams received little support from his colleagues with the exception of Jim Heard, who was a new signing from Eastbourne Eagles. Heard collected 8 points, his evening's work including an excellent win over Trevor Redmond. In fact, he would have collected 11 points if he hadn't overslid on the last bend of his final ride.

Heard fell right in the path of Roy Taylor, who instinctively took corrective action. Taylor's machine reared onto one wheel, but he somehow brought it under control to finish in second place. Today, pulling wheelies seems to be common place, but not back then! Full result: Neath 50 (Redmond 8; Charlie Monk 8; Howdy Cornell 8; Jon Erskine 7; Taylor 7; Glyn Chandler 6; George Major 6) Stoke 28 (Adams 13; Heard 8; Colin Pratt 3; Eric Hockaday 2; Pete Jarman 1; Ron Sharp 1; Ray Harris 0).

In the second half racing Ken Adams had a terrific tussle with local lad Chris Julian before he eventually won the Telstar Trophy. In the absence of Roy Wedlake the sidecar racing swung in the favour of Tywardreath crew, Williams and Stephens. Pat Crawford of Saltash finished as runner up. Meanwhile, a collection for the injured Roy Wedlake totalled a sum of £26-2-8 (£26.13)

Around this period Williams, who was then working at Charlestown Engineering, part of E.C.L.P., asked Ken Westaway who worked at Heavy Transport on Par Moor Road whether he would be interested in a ride at the speedway. Westaway took the opportunity to partner Williams and was immediately hooked. Before long Ken's brother Dave Westaway had agreed to join the sidecars boys as well. We look at the sidecar boy's in some depth later.

The next match was a challenge between the Gulls and their Devon neighbours Exeter on 24 July, when a tight affair ended all-square. The star of the evening was the visiting rider clad in white leathers Alan Cowland, who rode five times in eight heats to score 9 points. Full result: St. Austell 39 (Chris Julian 10; Chris Blewett 7; Trevor Redmond 5; Roy Taylor 5; Glyn Chandler 4; Ray Wickett 4; George Major 4) Exeter 39 (Len Silver 11; Howdy Byford 9; Cowland 9; Pete Lansdale 4; Eric Howe 3; Francis Cann 2; Gordon Bailey 1)

The following week on 31 July it was back to Provincial League racing as Neath entertained Bradford and handed out a pasting. Tommy Roper was the only visitor to show any glimmer of hope for the Panthers. As a matter of fact, he set a new track record of 68.4 seconds in heat one, but it didn't last long since Roy Taylor shaved off 0.4 of a second in heat two, establishing a new best time for the circuit of 68.0 seconds dead.

One of the promising youngsters on display in this period was Jon Erskine. His father, Mike, not only rode at Rocky Park before the war but also at the Cornish Stadium when it opened it's gates. In his heyday Mike Erskine was a sensational rider at Wimbledon (1946-51) before going on to manage Southampton. Mike Erskine was the person who not only revolutionised speedway

Ray Wickett makes ready in the pits, photo Ron Bassett.

with his Staride machines, but also helped so many youngsters including Trevor Redmond when he came to England.

Full result: Neath 51 (Charlie Monk 9; Roy Taylor 9; Jon Erskine 9; Redmond 7; George Major 6; Howdy Cornell 6; Glyn Chandler 5) Bradford 27 (Roper 11; Geoff Pymar 8; Wal Morton 6; Reg Duval 1; Stuart Hickman 1; Dennis Jenkins 0; Ray Day 0).

On 7 August St. Austell's nearest rivals were in town, with Plymouth drawing the largest crowd of the season as some 4,000 folk entered the Par Moor turnstiles for the first leg of the Capstan Trophy. Wouldn't Trevor Redmond have loved to have 'turned the clock back' to see crowds at the Cornish Stadium when he was carving a name for himself as a rider with Aldershot? 'Those were the days!' he'd say.

The Gulls gave a good account of themselves to beat the Devils by 5 points. Some spirited riding, particularly from Plymouth skipper Cliff Cox kept his side in the match and with just two heats to go they trailed by only 3 points. However, with a win in the next heat St. Austell secured the match. Full result: St. Austell 40 (Charlie Monk 9; George Major 9; Howdy Cornell 8; Francis

Cann 7; Redmond 6, Jon Erskine 1; Glyn Chandler 0) Plymouth 35 (Cox 13; Jimmy Squibb 9; Chris Julian 7; Ray Wickett 2; Chris Blewett 2; Ivor Toms 1; Lewis Philp 1). With rain cascading down onto the track during the interval the second half racing was abandoned by the promotion for safety reasons.

Two nights later on Thursday 9 August the St. Austell side travelled to Pennycross Stadium for the second leg of Capstan Trophy against Plymouth. The home side just kept their nose in front and never let the lead slip from their grasp. St. Austell were only 3 points adrift.

Jimmy Squibb was top scorer for the homesters with 11 points and his time of 73.6 seconds in heat one wasn't equalled all evening. He was well supported by Chris Julian and Chris Blewett, who netted eight points each. Full result: Plymouth 40 (Squibb 11; Blewett 8; Julian 8; Eric Howe 7; Cliff Cox 5; Ray Wickett 1; Ivor Toms 0) St. Austell 37 (Trevor Redmond 9; Howdy Cornell 8; Charlie Monk 6; Jon Erskine 5; Glyn Chandler 4; George Major 3; Francis Cann 2.)

Welsh Dragons left to right: Freddie Powell, Roy Taylor, T.R., Jon Erskine and Glyn Chandler.

Ivor Toms and Lew Philp in the colours of Plymouth. Ivor fractured his leg riding at Plymouth in 1961 which sidelined him. He returned the following season to be a regular at Plymouth where changes became abundant. Lew Philp continued riding up until 1963 when he had a bad crash at Sheffield which finished his track career. (photo Eric Martyn)

The result gave the Gulls the narrowest of victories on aggregate as they triumphed 77-75. In the second half racing Jon Erskine certainly enjoyed himself, winning the Reserves' Scratch event and his heat of the Devil/Gull races, before going on to take the final from Jimmy Squibb, Chris Blewett Charlie Monk.

The Provincial League encounter against Newcastle was scheduled for the following week, but unfortunately fell victim to inclement weather. On 21 August, Neath's Provincial Riders' Championship qualifying round was run at Par Moor instead of the Abbey Stadium. Plymouth captain Cliff Cox won the meeting with a 15-point maximum. With it the Bristol-born rider won the honour of a place in the final at Belle Vue on 22 September. Cox who became a firm favourite with the Devils' supporters, was helped in the pits by his friend and spanner-man Vic Skinner. Many fans were devastated when Plymouth closed at the end of the season.

Behind him, second place was shared between three riders all on twelve points, namely Glyn Chandler, Charlie Monk and Trevor Redmond. The meeting had its share of controversy because Chris Blewett collided with pal Chris

Julian in heat two. Julian fell on the inside of the last bend and was sent to hospital for observation. However, he later returned to the meeting to record two more third places. Meanwhile Blewett was disqualified from the re-run, and again fell in his next heat whilst challenging Ross Gilbertson. Full result: Cox 15; Chandler 12; Monk 12; Redmond 12; Jon Erskine 11; Gilbertson 9; Geoff Mudge 9; Howdy Cornell 6; Roy Taylor (reserve) 6; George Major (reserve) 6; Eric Howe 5; Ernie Baker 5; Clive Hitch 4; Francis Cann 3; Julian 2; Derek Timms 2; Ray Wickett 0; Chris Blewett 0. In the sidecar racing Phil Williams won convincingly from Alan Rowe and Eric Roberts.

The next event at Par Moor was a Three-Team Tournament between the Midlands, Cornwall and Wales on 28 August, as Trevor Redmond again proved he had a canny way of throwing a meeting together.

The man of the evening was Redruth's Chris Blewett, who collected victories in each of his first three rides and was the only man to beat Ken Adams, the Stoke captain. The unluckiest man on the night was George Major, who started well with 8 points from three rides before disaster struck! He lined up on the inside gate for his fourth ride and was set to speed away when his engine disintegrated in a cloud of sparks and black smoke. Major, who was drafted into the Midlands Select, had been a stalwart competitor, particularly when they were without Pete Jarman and only tracked a three-man team. Meanwhile, Roy Taylor's luck wasn't good either, as he was dogged by injury problems and only finished one race. Blewett, always an unpredictable rider, fell in his fourth heat. Despite crashing heavily, he was helped back to the pits amidst huge applause from the crowd.

Full result: Cornwall 26 (Blewett 9; Chris Julian 9; Redmond 7; Taylor 1); Midlands 25 (Adams 14; Major 8; Colin Pratt 3; Jarman DNA); Wales 22 (Howdy Cornell 8; Charlie Monk 7; Francis Cann 5; Glyn Chandler 2). In the Big Four event in the second half, Adams eventually took victory after a good scrap with Redmond. Aside from that, Exeter's Francis Cann won the Stars and Stripes race, while Eric Roberts took the sidecar spoils, winning heat one and the Scratch race.

Many folk have asked about cycle speedway in the area. Well, a decade before St. Austell had seen a very successful league programme operated in the Clay Country villages. Regrettably, by this time local cycle-speedway was beginning to wane. Not deterred in other areas of the country they rode week in, week out. East Anglia being cycle speedster heaven!

For those who remember Gordon Parkins promoting at Plymouth, you may not know he also managed the Norwich side. In 1962 his son, Mike won the World Cycle-Speedway Championship at Hamilton Park.

On the odd occasion Stan Stevens made a guest appearance for The Gulls. Stan was a rider who had done the rounds including riding at Rayleigh, Cradley and Southampton. Many years later he teamed up again with Chris Julian at Mildenhall.

On 5 September it was a chance to restage the rained off meeting against Newcastle, with the Neath side continuing their unbeaten run to win by 10 points in what was the last meeting of the season at Par Moor. The Provincial League undertaking had its shaky moments, but the team still finished as runners-up to Poole in the final table. Full result: Neath 44 (George Major 11; Roy Taylor 10; Jon Erskine 8; Trevor Redmond 8; Charlie Monk 5; Glyn Chandler 2) Newcastle 34 (Brian Craven 14; Bill Andrew 10; Vic Lonsdale 4; Peter Sampson 3; Gil Goldfinch 1; Mike Watkin 1; George Glenn 1).

The Speedway Queen for 1962 was selected on the final evening of the season. Fifteen-year-old Sonia Faulds from Coombe Farm, Bodmin was the winner of the contest. The large crowd was heartened by news that although the Abbey Stadium project hadn't seen sufficient numbers of the paying public enter through the turnstiles, Par Moor was still a viable alternative and would be considered for Provincial League racing the following season.

On 7 September the Neath/St. Austell side travelled up to the Old Meadowbank Stadium in Edinburgh. The visitors certainly put the wind up the home side in heat one, with Roy Taylor and Trevor Redmond racing to a 5-1 victory By heat 5 the teams were level on 15 points apiece. It was a close match and again after ten races the sides were evenly poised on 30 points each. Heat 11 was crucial as Redmond and Taylor aimed to outpoint the home duo of Alf Wells and George Hunter.

It was George Hunter who duly led from the gate with Redmond right on his tail. Misfortune saw Taylor pull over with machine troubles and the Monarchs went on to collect a good 4-2 win. Heat twelve was subsequently shared, leaving Edinburgh just 2 points to the good going into the last race of night. There was to be no fairytale for the long distance visitors though, since the on form Wayne Briggs made a tremendous start and was supported by Hunter, leaving Redmond to settle for third position as the Monarchs posted a 42-36 success.

Neath ended the season as Provincial League Runners-up. Cyril Hart wrote

Jon Erskine in the nineties at Claycountry Moto Parc with friend Alby Golden, the former Southampton rider was teamster with Jon at Newport. Photo Ron Bassett

of Trevor Redmond, "He created something out of nothing, put a team together, on a strange track, rode with them, captained them, managed them and convinced them that they were better than any other crowd." Hart described the team as 'nobodies' but the author thinks this is a reference to being virtually unknown riders.

At the end of the season Neath's Charlie Monk returned home to Australia. Also taking a trip 'down under' was 'Brit' Mike Broadbank from Swindon who ten days before Christmas won the Australian National Championship at Rockhampton.

Away from the track medical science was moving ahead by leaps and bounds helping people in motorcycling and everyday life. Lasers were used in eye surgery for the very first time. In the twenty-first century this technique is common place.

1963
A return to league racing

People remember certain years in history for different reasons. For those who enthuse over the space race, they will remember 1963 because of the exploits of Valentina Tereshkova. She was the first woman into space. For those who are politically minded, it was the year when U.S. President John Fitzgerald Kennedy was assassinated. In medicine an American surgeon attempted a liver transplant on a three year old boy. Sadly the little lad died. This pioneering operation would ultimately save many lives in later decades. On the music scene, 'Beatlemania' was sweeping Britain. 'The Fab Four' released 'She Loves You', which became Britain's best selling single with 1.6 million copies sold in the U.K. alone. For some local folk they were thrilled they could go and support their local speedway club the St. Austell Gulls in the Provincial League. An evening watching the brave and gutsy Chris Julian riding was indeed exciting!

Memories of Par Moor are abundant for local people, but they are held dear to folk from further afield also. Tony Oxford, a speedway fan and collector from Ashford in Kent, saw his first speedway at the Cornish Stadium. It made such a lasting impression that he was hooked and has been ever since. He takes up the story, thus: "My friend and I were just eighteen years of age and had watched Kent grass-track racing for two years. We were always impressed by two visiting riders who hailed from Cornwall their names were Chris Julian and Adrian Kessell. The lads from Cornwall were 'really good' so in the summer of 1963 riding my new Cotton 250cc Continental we set off for the sunny Duchy."

"It took us ten hours on what you could only describe as poor roads in those days. We stayed in a bed and breakfast in the town and explored the area. I remember riding up Mevagissey hill out of the village with a terrier nipping at my mate's heels as I urged the Cotton to go faster! Our first speedway meeting was a match at St. Austell against the Middlesbrough Bears. Eric Boocock was riding for the Bears then. Of course Ray Cresp, Trevor Redmond and Chris

Julian all rode for the home side as regulars that season.' Tony concluded: 'As the tapes went up we were impressed by the speed, the sport was thrilling, and by the end of the meeting we were both hooked! I'm now sixty-three years of age and it's still in the blood. We became West Ham and Hackney regulars until they closed down. Now we watch wherever we can!"

It was only January and the speculation in the press went along the lines of 'what was Trevor Redmond going to do?' Redmond's name was linked with that of Exeter's Francis Cann, who developed a close relationship with T.R. during the open years at Par Moor. It was also apparent Redmond was on the chase for Plymouth riders Chris Julian and Chris Blewett, with the former being subject to Control Board allocation. The only doubtful rider for a new Cornish side was Howdy Cornell, who had injured a wrist in the latter part of 1962. Speedway Star and News praised the St. Austell track, which had been designed by Jack Parker, Bill Kitchen and Vic Duggan in the late 1940s. They seemed hopeful that league status could return to Cornwall.

In February, Trevor Redmond attended the Provincial League Promoters' Convention at Poole. He said he would like to promote, whilst also continuing to ride. The Provincial League was inaugurated with the idea of giving the junior riders an outlet.

This it had definitely done, giving riders like David Dodd (Liverpool), Chris Julian (Bristol), Geoff Mudge (Poole), Stan Stevens (Rayleigh) and Pete Jarman (Stoke) their chance to break into a tough sport. Thus, the virility and pioneering spirit of the Provincial League had been born.

On 2 February, the Speedway Star & News announced the retirement of Exeter's Francis Cann. Prior to joining the Falcons, Trevor Redmond had made good use of Cann at Par Moor, where he demonstrated he had considerable talent. In 1961, Cann was duly snapped up by his local club and averaged over 5 points per match, having amassed a huge tally of bonus points. He was a good partner to Pete Lansdale and gelled well with the young Alan Cowland. With Lansdale retiring too, Exeter lost a good pairing from their side. Fans pondered the question. "Were they to be lured back?"

Rick Eldon expressed his empathy with Trevor Redmond's style of humour in a 1963 article. T.R. realised he had problems with the track at Par Moor so he dashed to the telephone and dialled the fire brigade. The Fire Station was in Bodmin Road in those days, the old building had served the town since 1939. In 2006 it was demolished to make way for additional town parking. Needless to say nothing was on fire, but T.R. wanted them to damp down the extremely dry track. A few nights later Redmond had travelled to Edinburgh with his Neath team to be greeted with torrential rain. He said: 'Why don't you ring the fire brigade to pump the water off the track?' This was a typical comment from the reigning Scottish Champion!

During the winter break it had been announced that Glyn Chandler would accompany Lew Coffin and Ray Harris to ride in Bremen and Oldenberg in May.

Meanwhile, the jungle drums were suggesting a Good Friday start for league racing by the Cornish promotion. Lo and behold it was to be an away match at Edinburgh on 27 April, which would start the ball rolling for the new season. With less than a month to go to the start of a new campaign Trevor Redmond released the exciting news that he was going to bring Australian Ray Cresp to Cornwall.

The incoming rider would be brought in to replace Howdy Cornell, who had announced his intention to stay in South Africa. Coincidentally, Cresp, throughout March 1963, raced on the touring car circuits of South Africa, driving a Cooper Climax. He was born in Melbourne, Victoria on 25 August 1928 and had been brought up on a farm with four brothers and five sisters. His initial rides had occurred at Melbourne in 1954 and he duly arrived in England two years later, becoming a real star with Wembley. Later, at Poole in 1959, he was a prolific scorer and actually topped his side's end-of-season scorechart with 143 points from sixteen matches.

Cresp had subsequently ridden for Ipswich and it was said at the time that teammate Eric Bason was devastated that the Aussie would not be returning to Suffolk because he always managed an average of over 8 points per match. The deal hinged on T.R. concluding an agreement with 'The Witches'. If he proved successful it was hoped Cresp would appear in a friendly against Exeter at the County Ground on April Fools Day. If anybody could lure him back from tarmac to shale it had to be Redmond!

However, there was a slight controversy at the time of the transfer because Cresp, a 1961 World Finalist in Malmo, a former boxer and a top Australian Test match rider, had previously been a heat leader in the National League. It meant Ray would be dropping down a league. Some interpreted the move by the Control Board as being lax, whilst others said it was a breakthrough and would make transfers easier in the future. As it turned out, Cresp's transfer wasn't sorted out in time for the season's opener.

St.Austell duly started their season at Exeter's County Ground in the Western Cup on Monday 1 April. The front cover of the match programme pictured Len Silver playing guitar. The meeting became a survival of the fittest. Trevor Redmond looked as sharp as ever, romping away with heat one. He continued in good form and recorded a superb 12-point maximum. Making his County Ground debut was Cliff Cox, the former Pennycross favourite, while Howdy Byford, Len Silver and Alan Cowland put in some solid scores for the home side. For the visitors it was only Chris Julian who supported Redmond. T.R. must have wondered what he would have done without the support of the Fraddon rider. Then there was the Cresp factor and his absence left the fans wondering what difference he might have made. With him missing the fixture, former Neath rider Jon Erskine was drafted into a reserve berth.

Full result: Exeter 45 (Silver 11; Cox 10; Byford 8; Cowland 7; Eric Howe 5; Bob Innocent 2; Dennis Day 2) St. Austell 32 (Redmond 12; Julian 8; Chris Blewett 4; George Major 4; Fred Powell 2; Glyn Chandler 2; Erskine 0). In the second half racing, Redmond and Blewett each won a heat in the Falcons' Stakes, although it was Cowland who went on to triumph in the final. Meanwhile Powell took the Reserves' Scurry ahead of Pete Selley and Innocent. On the downside, the second half was overshadowed by a serious crash involving Eric Howe, who was taken to hospital with serious head injuries and a broken wrist. Regrettably, he never returned to full fitness from the incident.

To give a little perception of 1963 prices, second hand speedway machines with four stud engines were fetching anything from £75 to £100. A box of football or speedway programmes would cost 10 shillings (50 pence). Speedway Star & News magazine was selling for one shilling a week (10 pence). I bet you are beginning to think of what you were earning when you started your occupation! In 1973 when the author started work he was earning £11 per week.

On the 12 April George Major made his debut for Swindon, he only rode a dozen meetings for 'The Robins' with moderate success. St.Austell's league campaign finally got underway at Long Eaton on Tuesday 16 April. The Nottinghamshire track was also returning to league racing after an absence of a few years and in a great start Charlie Monk broke the old track record in the very first heat. The visitors put in a plucky performance and were ahead by 8 points after heat nine. The Archers' supporters were thrilled though in heat ten, when Jon Erskine and Gil Goldfinch blasted their way to the front and team rode to

EXETER SPEEDWAY

EXETER v. ST. AUSTELL
(WESTERN CUP)
MONDAY, APRIL 1, 1963

OFFICIAL PROGRAMME NINEPENCE

Exeter speedway programme Western Cup tie 1st.April '63. Note Len Silver is on guitar.

keep George Major at bay. Although the Archers drew each of the last two heats it wasn't enough to deny the Cornish side a memorable victory. Full result: Long Eaton 38 (Monk 11; Erskine 9; Bluey Scott 6; Goldfinch 4; Slant Payling 3; Ken Vale 3; Vic White 2.) St. Austell 40 (Chris Julian 10; Chris Blewett 7; Trevor Redmond 6; Glyn Chandler 6; Bob Warner 4; Major 4; Fred Powell 3). In the second half racing Erskine had his revenge on old friend Redmond, beating him in the Jed Stone Tankard final.

A brief northern sojourn beckoned for the Cornish club. It meant a journey to Middlesbrough, before going the extra mile to Edinburgh. George Major explained how Trevor Redmond had asked whether he could take up all the bikes in his van, as he himself had to fly up on business. The van T.R. owned was a Ford Thames but it had done a lot of miles. It had a column change gearshift, which was well worn. If you changed gear a bit too quick the lever would jam between the gears. To free it off you had to crawl underneath and prise it out with a screwdriver.

George said it was the longest journey he ever had! Before George left, T.R. said he had booked them into a hotel and gave them a slip of paper with the address. When they arrived at their destination they found their hotel was the Y.M.C.A.

It wasn't done to save the lads the bother of booking, it was done to save T.R. a fortune on expenses. George continued, "On another trip North of the border we only had one meeting, so Trevor decided to take us all by train and a lorry would pick us up from the station. It all worked out well going up, but when we got on the night train to come back it was packed. By the time we had loaded the bikes, there wasn't a seat left anywhere. "Don't worry" said Trevor, "We will use a first class compartment."

About half an hour into the journey the ticket collector came in and said we would have to upgrade our tickets. "That's okay mate" said Trevor. He flashed a couple of quid and said, "Stick this in your pocket." Of course the ticket inspector was having none of it, muttering under his breath "More than my job's worth." He ordered us out securing the compartment by locking the door. They were left in the train corridor.

The riders tried to lie down in the corridor but people kept trying to walk past and to make matters worse there was some sort of rail accident ahead on the line. They stood for two hours before being diverted half way around Britain. It took what seemed to be forever to reach London, George said, "We

Chris Julian leads the way at Middleborough 25 April 1963.

laughed about it afterwards but at the time it wasn't funny. We were always wondering what scheme Trevor would dream up next."

The Middlesborough Bears pleased their home supporters on 25 April with a good win over the Gulls. Eric Boocock rode magnificently to score 11 points, while another Teesside favourite, Brian McKeown, tore around the track to record 10 points from four outings. Redruth's Chris Blewett, ever the trier, hit mechanical gremlins in his first heat but won all his further races. The Gulls certainly weren't disgraced, it wasn't like the village of Troon knocking up a cricket score. The match result was Middlesborough 45, St.Austell 33.

Full result: Middlesbrough 45 (Eric Boocock 11; McKeown 10; Clive Hitch 8; David Younghusband 7; Johnny Fitzpatrick 4; Kevin Torpie 3; Eric Boothroyd 2) St. Austell 33 (Chris Blewett 9; Trevor Redmond 8; Chris Julian 7; Glyn Chandler 3; George Major 3; Fred Powell 2; Ray Wickett 1) Middlesbrough were obviously impressed with Chris Julian, as they awarded him 'The Rider of Night trophy'.

The next evening saw a tough encounter at the Old Meadowbank Stadium. The track was greasy and the visitors made lots of friends by putting in some really gritty performances. Trevor Redmond led by example to score 12 points, giving his new crew every incentive. Doug Templeton and Dudley McKean were both fallers in heat one, but were able to continue. Chris Blewett again showed his promise as a high flyer by recording a win in heat three and a couple of second places. Blewett, who had done his National Service in the R.A.F., was quite an all round sports person because he boxed in the services and also played rugby union on the wing. The Scottish outfit's reserve Ken Cameron did his bit by notching six points from three rides as his side inflicted a 10-point defeat on the Gulls. The result was a disappointment as the tail-enders didn't grab the odd point when needed.

The full result: Edinburgh 44 (D. Templeton 10; Willie Templeton 9; Wayne Briggs 7; George Hunter 7; Cameron 6; Alf Wells 4; McKean 1) St. Austell 34(Redmond 12; Blewett 7; Chris Julian 6; George Major 4; Ray Wickett 4; Glyn Chandler 1; Fred Powell 0.)

The next leg of the mini-tour was back down to London to the Old Kent Road to face New Cross on 30 April. This wasn't a league encounter, but a first round tie in the Knock-Out Cup. St. Austell were still without Ray Cresp, but fielded unsung riders Bob Warner and Ray Wickett instead. The bearded Jimmy Squibb rode a blinder for the home side, scoring a wonderful 15-point

Ray in action at Meadowbank, Edinburgh,
photos John Hanney, Newcastle upon Tyne.

maximum. Meanwhile, Bobby Dugard excelled with 14 points and Reg Reeves tally was 11. Trevor Redmond proved yet again to be the mainstay for the Gulls, but they lost on this occasion by 21 points. The final scoreline said it all, despite some typically hair-raising riding from Chris Blewett. TR, the wily Kiwi, had his revenge over Dugard for an earlier defeat in a last heat scrap of the night. Redmond also put on a good show in the Silver Sash Match Race, but it was Squibb who eventually came out on top. Full result: New Cross 58 (Squibb 15; Dugard 14; Reeves 11; Des Lukehurst 7; Geoff Penniket 6; Stan Stevens 6; Eddie Reeves 0). St. Austell 37 (Trevor Redmond 14, Chris Julian 8; Chris Blewett 5; Glyn Chandler 4; George Major 3; Bob Warner 3; Ray Wickett 0).

On 11 May the Gulls' travelled to the Midlands to face Cradley Heath in a Provincial League fixture. Hero of the hour for the home side was Ivor Brown, who did all the hard work to rescue the Heathens from defeat. He completed a marvellous 15-point maximum in the final heat of the night to clinch a draw. Meanwhile, Ray Cresp made his debut for the St. Austell club, but could only muster 3 points. However, he did show his gating ability as he was leading two races when each time he shed a chain. Maybe Lady Luck just wasn't shining! The meeting wasn't without controversy, with Chris Blewett twice featuring in a commotion. Following heat ten, tempers got very heated because he rode Alan Totney into the fence yards from the line, costing Cradley a valuable point. Not one to do things by halves, Blewett courted controversy again in the second half, when he won the Scratch Race final, from which Brown had been

A speedway advertising board at Par Station in 1963 (thanks to Fred Paul)

excluded. The story told at the time was Brown went mad and took the law into his own hands by thumping Blewett upon his return to the pits area. Full result below: Cradley Heath 36 (Brown 15; Derek Timms 6; Harry Bastable 5; John Hart 5; John Belcher 3; Alan Totney 2; Jim Westwood 0) St. Austell 36 (Trevor Redmond 9; Glyn Chandler 8; Chris Julian 8; George Major 4; Cresp 3; Blewett 2; Ray Wickett 2). St. Austell were next in action on 20 May, when they took on the might of the 'Exeter Falcons' on their fast home 'County Ground' track. The Falcons in their eighth match of the season brought in Gordon Bailey as reserve, but it was Pat Flanagan who shone, giving the big boys plenty of support. The match was one the Cornish club would prefer to forget due to a nasty injury sustained by Chris Blewett. The man from Redruth had been riding like a trooper and netted 6 points from three rides. Then disaster struck as he parted company from his machine, which came within inches of going over the steel fence. Chris Blewett lay on the track holding his left arm, prior to being taken to hospital with a suspected double fracture. Chris Julian top scored for 'The Gulls' with 8 points and was steadily settling into the side and learning the tricks of the track! Incidentally Trevor Redmond's photograph appeared on the programme cover for this meeting. Full result: Exeter 47 (Len Silver 12; Alan Cowland 10; Cliff Cox 7; Pat Flanagan 6; Howdy Byford 6; Dennis Day 6; Bailey 0) St. Austell 31 (Julian 8; Trevor Redmond 6; Blewett 6; Ray Cresp 5; Glyn Chandler 3; Ray Wickett 2; George Major 1).

The following evening the Gulls entertained Poole in a Western Cup match. Young Australian George Summers was called upon to join the side at short notice. He was brought in to replace the injured Chris Blewett. St. Austell went on to open their home programme with a good win over the Pirates in front of a fair sized crowd. Admission prices varied between 2/- and 5/- with on-site refreshments. The Gulls new signing Ray Cresp did the bulk of the scoring with 10 points, being supported by the bearded George Major with 9. Preston Pote a loyal 'Gulls' supporter for many years who travelled from the Liskeard area commented that Ray Cresp was a good rider but had quite a 'laid back personality'. Preston continued, "When Ray Cresp and George Major were paired together their team riding was brilliant, something you don't forget."

George Major concurred, he said, "I loved the St.Austell oval, for me it was the perfect speedway track. I was paired with Ray Cresp and we rode really well together. I think we were the highest scoring pair in the League that year. We both qualified for the Provincial League Riders Final. If I remember correctly I think there were thirteen teams and Ray was the top scorer. They took the next three highest average riders, of which I was one."

Skipper Geoff Mudge and teammate Ross Gilbertson scored well for the visitors, but the two were not supported from the ranks. The unusual twist to the meeting was that Poole's reserve Pete Munday bagged 8 points. Full result: St. Austell 41 (Cresp 10; Major 9; Glyn Chandler 8; Trevor Redmond 7; Chris Julian 4; Ray Wickett 3; Summers 0) Poole 37 (Mudge 12; Gilbertson 11; Munday 8; Pete Smith 4; Norman Strachan 2; Lewis Philp 0; Stuart Wallace 0). Capping a fine night for Gilbertson, he went on to win the Carlyon Cup in the second half.

Ray Cresp chats with pusher and son sorry didn't recognize who it is! Photo Ron Bassett.

Riders are (left to right) Ray Cresp, Glyn Chandler, Freddie Powell (reporter Graham Hambly) front Trevor Redmond (capt) George Major, Ray Wickett and Chris Julian. Photo courtesy of Speedway Surveys

On Saturday 25 May, the St. Austell team travelled to Sun Street Stadium in Hanley to face Stoke, with home promoter Reg Fearman extending a warm welcome to the Gulls in his programme notes. Unfortunately, the Cornish side was without Chris Blewett, his place being taken by teammate and friend Ray Wickett. Although the visitors drew heats five, seven and twelve, they struggled to make their mark on the meeting as the Potters really hit them where it hurts. Full result: Stoke 50 (Peter Jarman 12; Eric Hockaday 10; Colin Pratt 9; Ken Adams 6; Roy Bowers 6; Kid Bodie 5; Ron Sharp 2) St. Austell 26 (Ray Cresp 10; Trevor Redmond 6; Chris Julian 6; George Major 3; Glyn Chandler 1; Ray Wickett 0; Fred Powell 0).

The St.Austell Gulls team photograph was not published in Speedway Star and News until 31st.August. A mystery surrounded the photograph for some enthusiasts. Was there a new team manager pictured on the right of the back row? The well-known journalist Graham Hambly who wrote for The Western Morning News and the Evening Herald was asked to join the line up by Trevor Redmond. Graham had travelled to the meeting at the old Stoke track with Chris Julian. Some forty years later the mystery is solved the young man in the rain-coat is indeed the announcer/presenter at both the Claycountry Moto Parc and the St.Boniface Arena.

Tuesday 28 May saw the rematch of near neighbours St. Austell and Exeter in a Provincial League fixture at Par Moor. The track was wet, which made riding treacherous. Exeter's superior team riding gave them the victory on the night, despite the loss of Howdy Byford in heat five. The visiting rider had hit the front and looked to be on his way to victory, but overslid and fell. Chris Julian was unable to avoid the stricken rider and ran over his arm, before falling on the wet track himself. The Exeter Falcons went on to win the match with a maximum from their captain Len Silver. Full result: St. Austell 33 (George Major 10; Glyn Chandler 9; Trevor Redmond 6; Julian 3; Ray Cresp 3; Ray Wickett 2; Fred Powell 0) Exeter 44 (Silver 12; Alan Cowland 10; Dennis Day 8; Cliff Cox 5; Pat Flanagan 5; Byford 3; Gordon Bailey 1). The weather conditions worsened, putting paid to the second half racing. Trevor Redmond did his utmost to scotch rumours that Glyn Chandler was moving to Cradley. It appeared the inquiry probably came from the Heathens manager Roy Moreton.

On Whit Monday 3 June, the Gulls faced New Cross in an afternoon league encounter at the Cornish Stadium, which commenced at 3.15 p.m. Maximums by Ray Cresp, Glyn Chandler (his first full-house) and Chris Julian saw the home side coasting to victory. Indeed, by heat eight the Gulls had opened up a 31-11 advantage. In an effort to make up the arrears, the Rangers brought in Bob Dugard as a tactical substitute and he duly netted the visitors' only win of the afternoon. Aside from Dugard, only Jimmy Squibb kept the flag flying for the Londoners. Full result: St. Austell 53 (Chandler 12; Cresp 12; Julian 12; George Major 6; Trevor Redmond 5; Bob Warner 5; Ray Wickett 1) New Cross 25 (Squibb 10; Bob Dugard 8; Stan Stevens 4; Des Lukehurst 1; Eddie Reeves 1; Terry Stone 1; Geoff Penniket 0).

The press at the time brought to the public's attention in a quick phrase 'look out for the speedy Martyn'. They were obviously pleased with Eric Martyn, the local lad who won the Carnival Cowboys race in the second half, beating both Eric Roberts and Reg Hawken.

In the sidecar racing, the recently married Roy Wedlake broke off his honeymoon to win the scratch event ahead of Pat Crawford and Johnny Payton.

Roy who was forty years of age, married his sweetheart Josephine. It was obvious to any bystander over the years that Jo and Roy were very much soul mates. Meanwhile in the handicap race Wedlake had far too much ground to make up, this allowed Pat Crawford his chance to enjoy the victory. Incidentally

Speedway rider Ivor Toms with friend and motorcycle proprietor Cyril Jacobs prepare for a trials event.

two years later Jo and Roy were blessed with a son who they named Andrew. Yes he rode in a sidecar at a very young age! In the Whitsun Trophy, Squibb won the final from Cresp and Julian.

On 4 June, the Gulls travelled to Manor Park, London for the return match with New Cross, who were run by Wally Mawdsley and Pete Lansdale at the time. Eddie Reeves was drafted into the Rangers side in place of his father, Reg, while Bob Warner continued in the St. Austell line-up instead of Roy Taylor. Following a shared opening race the second heat proved to be quite exciting. Glyn Chandler hit the front and was chased by Bobby Dugard, who did everything he could to unsettle the young Gull. However, Chandler hung on to win and with Chris Julian in third place the visitors collected a 4-2.

With the next three heats drawn, it remained close. Julian challenged Jimmy Squibb whilst he was leading in heat five, setting hearts fluttering. Trevor Redmond won heat six in the fastest time of the night, 62.0 seconds. Putting it in context though his time was still almost 3 seconds outside the track record.

New Cross Speedway programme cover 4 June 1963.

In heat nine, Warner crashed heavily and Redmond snapped his front forks. It was an unusual occurrence in speedway, but that gifted the homesters a 5-0. A good 4-2 from Julian and Chandler in heat eleven edged the visitors ahead by 3 points.

Heat twelve was shared, which left the deficit the same. The final race saw Squibb and Reeves pitched against Julian and George Major. In an exciting climax Squibb rode like a thing possessed, but then he did have Julian on his tail. Despite George Major falling, the 2 points from Julian won the match for the visitors. Full result: New Cross 38 (Dugard 13; Squibb 12; Stan Stevens 8; Lukehurst 2; Reeves 2; Terry Stone 1; Geoff Penniket 0) St. Austell 39 (Ray Cresp 9; Julian 8; Chandler 7; Redmond 7; Major 4; Warner 2; Ray Wickett 2). In the second half, Reeves won the Junior Scurry, while Squibb took the Rangers' Stakes final from Dugard.

During this time Trevor Redmond had attained the chairmanship of the Provincial League Promoters' Association and this would have ramifications for the Cornish club in the future.

The Gulls completed a busy stint of three meetings in as many days on 5 June, with a trip to Dorset to meet Poole in a Provincial League encounter. Unfortunately, both Trevor Redmond and Ray Cresp were hit with machine troubles when cruising to easy wins, with the two heats ending in draws instead of St. Austell advantages. For consistency Glyn Chandler was the man to beat; he took heats three and twelve, while also claiming second places in heats seven and ten. Although they didn't win everyone was full of praise for the visiting side. Full result: Poole 44 (Geoff Mudge 9; Norman Strachan 9; Ross Gilbertson 7; Tim Bungay 6; Tony Lewis 6; Pete Smith 4; Pete Munday 3) St. Austell 34 (Chandler 10; Cresp 8; Redmond 7; Chris Julian 5; George Major 3; Ray Wickett 1; Bob Warner 0). There was at least some consolation in the second half, with Cresp winning the Third Man Scratch Race, while Redmond triumphed in the Dorset Scurry.

On Tuesday 11 June some of the finest racing in a long while was witnessed at Par Moor. A large crowd gathered, rekindling shades of days gone by, to watch a World Championship qualification round. George Hunter emerged as the highest scorer on the night, while the diminutive John Hart was runner-up. The star of the evening was undoubtedly young gun John Dews, who rode for Sheffield. His full-throttle antics had spectators on the edge of their seats. Full result: Hunter 14; Hart 13; Dews 12; Trevor Redmond 12; Ray Cresp 11; Les

Owen 10; Harry Edwards 8; Clive Hitch 8; John Edwards 6; Mike Watkin 6; Rick France 5; Maury McDermott 4; Bill Powell 4; John Belcher 3; Bob Warner 3; John Mills 1; Reg Hawken 0.

Leading speedway writer Eric Linden wrote an interesting article at this time concerning Trevor Redmond's interest in taking speedway to Canada and Japan. T.R. who was the only rider, captain and promoter operating in the Provincial League, was also a representative on the Speedway Control Board. The enterprising Kiwi was quoted as saying: 'There has always been a spark of interest in Canada; now I see the spark glowing brighter with the possibility of sponsorship.' His plan was to take a touring team out to test the water in North America and then fly to Japan for the second stretch.

In the World Championship qualifying rounds former Pirate Ray Cresp recorded 11 points at Poole on 12 June. Top scorer with 15 points was Swindon high-flyer Brian Brett, who had spent a lot of time at the Cornish Stadium during the Open Years. The following evening Trevor Redmond was at Middlesbrough representing the club, but he could only manage equal fourth place with Pete Jarman on 11 points.

Home riders Eric Boocock and Eric Boothroyd, along with Southampton's Peter Vandenberg all finished level at the top on 14 points apiece. That same evening Glyn Chandler and George Major were in action at Owlerton, Sheffield. Tigers front man, Jack Kitchen was the star of the show with a maximum tally of 15 points, while Clive Featherby also impressed with a tally of 12. The St. Austell representatives finished in the middle order of scores, Major netting 8 points and Chandler just 4.

Also, on 14 June Ray Wickett and Lewis Philp rode at the Wessex Stadium for Weymouth. The home line-up included Lew Coffin, Bob Hughes, Ken Vale, John McGill and Bill Billman, with the newly named Royals enjoying a good evening as they defeated Eastbourne 47-31. Coffin, the Weymouth skipper, was building a big name for himself in grass-track racing.

At this time Lew was Southern Centre 250cc and 350cc Champion, the Three Counties Show Challenge Cup winner, Withington Show Challenge Trophy winner and Somerset Champion. Briefly going back to the match against 'The Eagles' Wickett was joint top scorer with Hughes, both speedsters notching 11 points. Later in the season, Wickett top scored again when the Weymouth side claimed a 44-34 victory over a Midlands select. These matches certainly gave him the valuable riding experience he needed.

A rare shot of Ray Wickett.

On 18 June the Gulls entertained their 'arch rivals' Exeter in a Provincial League match. There were never more than 4 points between the teams, making it an exciting spectacle for the fans. A brilliant piece of competitive speedway from this match was etched in the minds of spectators when Bob Warner took the spoils in heat eight. He overcame a bad start to beautifully come through from third to first, initially overtaking Pat Flanagan, before taking Dennis Day on the inside. In heat 9, Len Silver was unlucky when he lost ground after clipping the safety fence on the outside while trying to take the lead from Chris Julian. He ended up finishing in third place, but despite his misfortune the visitors continued to fight for every point.

Trevor Redmond was back to his old form with eleven points and he received good support from Fraddon's never-give-an-inch Chris Julian, who tallied ten. Indeed, it was the home duo that secured victory with a spot of brilliant team riding in the final heat. Meanwhile, Ray Wickett rode much better than his one point suggested, he was indeed a 'trier'. Exeter's performance included the strong comeback of Francis Cann, who bagged nine valuable points.

Although Alan Cowland, Len Silver and Pete Lansdale also rode well, it would be wrong to underestimate the plucky effort by T.R.'s team. The scores were close with only four points separating the sides. Full result: St. Austell 41 (Trevor Redmond 11; Chris Julian 10; Ray Cresp 9; Glyn Chandler 5; Bob Warner 4; George Major 1; Wickett 1) Exeter 37 (Francis Cann 9; Alan Cowland 7; Len Silver 7; Pete Lansdale 7; Cliff Cox 4; Day 2; Pat Flanagan 1).

There was a brief delay in the second half racing due to an unusual turn of events. Before the start of the Pixie final, Silver and Julian went out on to the track in preparation to race, however, the other participants, Cresp and Chandler just couldn't be found. They were finally located in the pits in Chandler's van listening to commentary on the boxing bout between Henry Cooper and Cassius Clay!

During the contest, Cooper, the British Heavyweight Champion, became the first fighter to knock the young Clay to the canvas. Of course, Clay later became known as Muhammed Ali and went on to make boxing history. Ali became one of the most famous names of the twentieth century. Sadly the former fighter has developed Parkinson's Disease. Finally, in the Pixie final, Julian raced away to victory ahead of Cresp and Chandler.

St. Austell's next team match took them to Dudley Wood to face Cradley Heath in the first leg of the Midland/Cornish Trophy on 22 June. Young John Hart showed he was the master of the circuit, securing five race wins. Mean-

Trevor Redmond at
Cornish Stadium,
photo R.Bassett.

while, Geoff Mudge stood in for Ivor Brown who was riding at Edinburgh and as always, put on a good display to bag ten points.

Ray Cresp proved he was settling to the Provincial League racing and took three wins. Trevor Redmond showed he could come from the back when he needed to, winning heat four in grand style after passing Mudge and Alan Totney. If anything, it was inconsistency that let the side down as George Major recorded six points from two rides, then only registered a further two points from his three other rides. In heat ten he recorded the fastest time of the night, 72.6 seconds, to put the Gulls on even terms at 30-30. After the interval though, the visitors let a few races slip away and after fourteen heats they were eight points in arrears. Despite this, a 5-1 in heat fifteen from Cresp and Major gave the Gulls a chance to level the match. However, the Gulls were to be denied the spoils by that man Hart, for despite being pushed hard by Redmond, the home man took his fifth win of the night.

Full result: Cradley Heath 50 (Hart 15; Mudge 10; Totney 8; Harry Bastable 6; Derek Timms 6; John Edwards 5; John Belcher 0) St. Austell 46 (Cresp 12; Redmond 12; Major 8; Chris Julian 7; Glyn Chandler 5; Bob Warner 1; Ray Wickett 1). In the second half, Chandler and Major recorded wins, the latter's coming in the final of the intriguingly entitled 'Pluck the Gulls Scratch Race'. Meanwhile, it was former 1950s Gull Derek Timms who won the Reserves' Match Race. Regrettably, bad luck was to follow St. Austell back to Cornwall.

On Tuesday 25 June, the Gulls met Sheffield and were taken a little by surprise by the South Yorkshire outfit, although both Ray Cresp and Glyn Chandler had a poor night. Jack Kitchen, who went through the card to score a maximum, instigated St. Austell's downfall. There was a brilliant tactical ride by Chris Julian in heat nine, when he defeated visiting skipper Clive Featherby. The exciting home rider was holding the advantage, but as he came into the pit straight for his last lap 'Feathers' went inside to take the lead. Going into the third bend, Julian eased back the throttle before storming inside his opponent who was drifting wide on the fourth bend. Full praise was also due to George Major, who was only beaten by Kitchen and Featherby on the night. The Gulls needed a 5-1 from the last heat to snatch a draw after Tommy Roper and John Dews had increased the Tigers' lead to 4 points. It wasn't to be as Kitchen won the race, despite close attention from T.R.and Julian who were on his tail throughout. Full result: St. Austell 37 (Major 9; Redmond 7; Julian 7; Chandler 5; Ray Cresp 5; Bob Warner 2; Ray Wickett 2) Sheffield 41 (Kitchen

Cradley Heath programme cover 22 June 1963.

FIXTURES

				Result
April 1	Away	Exeter	WC	32-45 lost
16	Away	Long Eaton	PL	38-40 won
25	Away	Middlesborough	CH	32-45 lost
27	Away	Edinburgh	PL	34-44 lost
30	Away	New Cross	KC	37-58 lost
May 11	Away	Cradley	PL	36-36 draw
20	Away	Exeter	PL	31-47 lost
21	Home	Poole	WC	41-37 won
25	Away	Stoke	PL	50-26 lost
28	Home	Exeter	WC	33-44 lost
June 3	Home	New Cross	PL	53-25 won
4	Away	New Cross	PL	39-38 won
5	Away	Poole	PL	44-34 lost
11	Home	World Champ.		G. Hunter
18	Home	Exeter	PL	41-37 won
25	Home	Sheffield	PL	
27	Away	Middlesborough	PL	*LOST RAINED OFF*
29	Away	Raleigh	PL	*WON*
July 2	Home	Poole	PL	
9	Home	Edinburgh	PL	
16	Home	Middlesborough	PL	
18	Away	Sheffield	PL	
23	Home	Newcastle	PL	
29	Away	Newcastle	PL	
30	Home	Stoke	PL	
Aug. 2	Away	Wolverhampton	PL	
6	Home	Cradley	PL	
13	Home	Britain v Overseas		
20	Home	Prov. Riders Champ.		
27	Home	Raleigh	PL	
Sept. 3	Home	Hackney Wick	PL	
10	Home	Wolverhampton	PL	
17	Home	Open	PL	
18	Away	Hackney	PL	
24	Home	Long Eaton	PL	

CORNISH STADIUM
ST AUSTELL

TUESDAY, 25th JUNE, 1963
AT 7.45 P.M.

Lucky
Programme

Nọ 1109

PROVINCIAL LEAGUE

ST. AUSTELL GULLS
v.
SHEFFIELD TIGERS

Official Souvenir Programme 9d.

W. & T. Saunders, Printers, St. Austell

Programme cover 25th June 1963.

12; Featherby 9; Roper 9; Alan Jay 7; Dews 2; Ron Bagley 2; Ken Hanscombe 0). Following the main event Chandler won the Pixies final ahead of Kitchen, which must have given him great satisfaction. In the Speedway Practice session, it was Eric Roberts who took victory from Eric Martyn and Reg Hawken.

Meanwhile, in the sidecars Phil Williams won the first race from Alan Rowe, before Pat Crawford was victorious in the handicap event, with Roy Wedlake and Williams struggling to make up the gap. In one heat Williams spun off the track on to the grass and wrestled with the machine. T.R. who had been standing on the football pitch now found he had an outfit with no brakes chasing him!

Another interesting story emerges from the Sheffield encounter at Cornish Stadium. Sheffield speedway fan Peter Singleton and his family used to have speedway holidays during this period based around League meetings. So they hired a caravan at Par Sands to enable them to visit both the Exeter and St.Austell tracks. They met up with Sheffield rider Clive Featherby who got into a spot of bother. He drove his Austin Metropolitan all the way to Cornwall only to find it wouldn't restart. The B.M.C. car was apparently notorious for this. Stuck on Par Sands car park Clive had to unload all the gear out of his boot to tap the petrol pump to clear the fault. If there wasn't a click you knew the pump was not functioning correctly. With it working Clive was away again! Clive Featherby was one of the Sheffield all time 'speedway greats' who packed in the fans at Owlerton. Frank Varey would always pay Clive an extra 'fiver' if he broke the track record.

On 29 June, the St. Austell team travelled to Rayleigh for a Provincial League match, tracking the same team that had lost to Sheffield a few evenings before.

They began brightly, with Glyn Chandler winning the opening heat and Trevor Redmond filling third place for a 4-2. The home captain Harry Edwards was second, while 1950s St. Austell teamster Maurice McDermott took a fall, although thankfully he wasn't hurt. The Gulls plugged away and were a commanding 16 points in front after heat nine. With three 4-2s of their own, Rayleigh started a fight-back albeit too late to salvage the situation and it was St. Austell who won due to a solid workman-like performance. In comparison, Rayleigh was a two-man team with the load spread between Stan Clark and Harry Edwards. Full result: Rayleigh 34 (Clark 12; Edwards 8; McDermott 6; Derek Strutt 5; Vic Ridgeon 2; Roy Bowers 1; Sandy McGillivray 0) St. Austell 44 (Chandler 12; George Major 9; Chris Julian 8; Redmond 6; Ray Cresp 5; Ray Wickett 2; Bob Warner 2)

Good news reached St.Austell that former Gulls' rider Francis Cann's wife Valerie had given birth to a baby boy. Also away from the track, Chris Blewett was still suffering considerable pain from his broken arm, which was taking time to recover. It was also rumored on the terraces that Trevor Redmond had approached Ivor Toms, with the idea of him making a return to solo speedway, the rider having prematurely retired from speedway after breaking his leg at Plymouth in 1961. Ivor Toms, who had also dabbled with sidecar racing, would have undoubtedly been an asset to the St.Austell Gulls if he found his old form.

On 1 July several St. Austell riders took part in the Jack Unstead Memorial Trophy at Exeter's County Ground. George Major, George Summers and Glyn Chandler all made the effort to take part. However, it was Len Silver who deservedly won the event with a 15-point maximum. This he did despite a nasty tangle with Jimmy Squibb in the final and decisive heat. Meanwhile, Cliff Cox

Eric Boothroyd who supported
Eric Boocock on the night,
photo courtesy of The Wright Wood
Collection, thanks to
John Somerville

rode well to bag 14 points and take runner-up spot, with Ross Gilbertson third on a tally of 13. Of the St. Austell contingent, Major was the leading performer with seven points, ahead of Chandler on five, and Summers two.

Regrettably, the home league match scheduled for 2 July against Poole was postponed due to torrential rain, which poured down for an hour and a half before start time. Two days later the away match at Middlesbrough was also hit by the bad weather. In spite of a very wet Cleveland Park circuit, the meeting still went ahead.

To say the least it was the fog which made the racing very 'tricky.' Home teamster Eric Boocock simply revelled in the wet, however, collecting a superb four-ride maximum. Close on Boocock's heels were Cornishman Chris Julian and Kiwi Trevor Redmond, who recorded scores of ten points, helping their side to a draw. The Gulls deserved to share the points on the night, due to their gritty determination in such atrocious conditions. The full result: Middlesbrough 39 (Boocock 12, Eric Booothroyd 7; Dave Younghusband 7; Johnny Fitzpatrick 6; Kevin Torpie 3; Clive Hitch 2; Allan Butterfield 2) St. Austell 39 (Redmond 10; Julian 10; George Major 9; Ray Cresp 4; Glyn Chandler 3; Ray Wickett 3; Bob Warner 0).

The Speedway Star and News described St. Austell's next home match on 9 July with the headline: 'Poor old Edinburgh! This headline was apt as the Gulls had cruised to an easy win over an injury stricken Monarchs side. It seemed crazy that the Scottish outfit had travelled to Cornwall so under strength, without George Hunter, Wayne Briggs, Willie Templeton and Red Monteith. Despite gigantic odds, the Monarchs did try hard. One could speculate that visiting promoter Ian Hoskins' face must have been pale after heat six. This had seen Doug Templeton crash with Aussie Ray Cresp, before being carried off on a stretcher. Thankfully, the plucky Templeton returned to ride, but did not score.

Full result: St. Austell 58 points(George Major 12; Chris Julian 12; Glyn Chandler 10; Ray Cresp 9; Trevor Redmond 8; Ray Wickett 5; Bob Warner 2) Edinburgh 19 points(Eric Eadon 5; Jimmy Tannock 4; Bill McMillan 4; Templeton 2; Bert Harkins 2; Dudley McKean 2; Ian Hart 0), In the second half racing, George Major beat Cliff Cox in the Woodbine West of England Match Race. Completing an excellent personal night, Major also won the Woodbine Trophy final from Chandler, Cresp and Julian. Finally, the Wills Consolation Race resulted in victory for Lewis Philp, with Bob Warner and Reg Hawken finishing second and third respectively.

On 13 July, Trevor Redmond rode in the Best Pairs Championship at Edinburgh against some tough opposition. It is important to remember in the old days that it took ten hours of non-stop driving to reach Edinburgh from Cornwall. T.R.was paired with Red Monteith, who unfortunately wasn't on his best form.

The winners after a dramatic run-off were home skipper Doug Templeton and his regular track partner Jimmy Tannock. They beat the Newcastle pair of Bob Duckworth and Mike Watkin, who were left behind almost from the gate. As it panned out, Watkin was forced to retire with engine problems. The biggest disappointment for the large crowd was Ivan Mauger. He arrived late to score 5 points from two rides. Results: 1st Templeton (11) and Tannock (7) = 18; 2nd Duckworth (14) and Watkin (4) = 18; 3rd Dudley McKean (11) and George Hunter (5) = 16; 4th Wayne Briggs (14) and Bert Harkins (1) = 15; 5th Redmond (8) and Monteith (5) = 13; 6th Mauger (5) and Bill McMillan (4) = 9.

George Major in the pits at Par Moor, photo Ron Bassett.

Trevor Redmond was in the news again, this time Eric Linden was quick to report 'the Kiwi's' revised plans for the winter. The two-way stretch to Canada and Japan was radically changed and instead, eight lucky riders would tour South Africa, probably riding at Cape Town, Kimberley and Bloemfontain. The next stop could be Johannesburg, followed by Pretoria and across the border to Bulawayo. They then planned to go on to Pietermaritzburg, finishing in Durban. Later the tour would go on to Australia, stopping at Perth, Adelaide, Melbourne and Sydney. Then the globetrotting riders would do at least two meetings in New Zealand, followed by Singapore or Bangkok. After Hong Kong it would be on to Japan, then Hawaii. The intention was that the tour would end in North America, probably in Canada as originally envisaged. Only T.R. knew whether he could make it a reality!

Tuesday 16 July saw the Gulls wrestle with Middlesbrough in a Provincial League match at Par Moor. The previous night Exeter had comfortably beaten the Bears 55-23, but during this match the visitors lost the very capable Eric Boothroyd after he had hit the fence whilst dicing with Cliff Cox. St.Austell were to repeat the defeat of 'The Bears', although the margin of victory was a lot less. The match was won for the home side by 'maximum man' Glyn Chandler, who received solid support from teammate George Major. The bearded rider, who was also enjoying rides at National League level with Oxford, was excluded in heat two, but still went on to win his other three rides. Full result: St. Austell 44 (Chandler 12; Major 9; Chris Julian 7; Ray Cresp 6; Ray Wickett

6; Trevor Redmond 3; Bob Warner 1) Middlesbrough 34 (Eric Boocock 10; Dave Younghusband 9; Johnny Fitzpatrick 7; Kevin Torpie 5; Lew Philp 3; Allan Butterfield 0; Clive Hitch 0). In the second half racing, Warner won the Junior Jamboree from Torpie and Philp.

Meanwhile, Major pipped Boocock to the line in the Big Four event and Cresp won the Scratch Race. The travelling never ends when you're a speedway rider! Next stop was Owlerton Stadium, Sheffield, home of the Tigers on 18 July. Regrettably though, the career of Lewis Philp was prematurely ended in this meeting, when he was involved in a serious accident and was taken to hospital, where he remained for several weeks. On the night of the accident, he was actually on the critical list. Chris Julian rode very well to top score for his side, although in two of his race wins his partner never finished. Clive Featherby and Tommy Roper glued the home side together that night as they took victory by a ten-point margin. During this period Frank Varey was packing in crowds of up to 6,000 people. Full result: Sheffield 44 (Featherby 11; Roper 11; Ron Bagley 8; John Dews 5; Alan Jay 4; Ken Hanscombe 3; Tony Robinson 2) St. Austell 34 (Julian 10; George Major 9; Ray Cresp 6; Glyn Chandler 5; Trevor Redmond 4; Ray Wickett 0; Lew Philp 0). Top Tiger of this era, Clive Featherby away from the track worked in the print industry.

Rain caused the second postponement of the season at the Cornish Stadium on 23 July. This time the visitors should have been Newcastle Diamonds, including Silver Sash holder Ivan Mauger. The former World Champion remembered the rain off. He said, "I was with the Newcastle team who travelled in a bus which was hired by Mike Parker. I think if I recall correctly, the bikes were also in the back of the bus. We had been to Rayleigh on Saturday, then into Devon to race at Exeter on Monday. St.Austell was Tuesday when the heaven's opened."

On Saturday 27 July, Trevor Redmond and Ray Cresp rode for the Overseas side against Great Britain at Edinburgh. T.R. got 'The Overseas' off the mark, combining with Charlie Monk for a good 5-1. The New Zealander rode by example and top scored for his side with 13 points. Ivan Mauger rode his socks off until his last two races, when he hit mechanical problems with his machine. Despite this, he still recorded a tally of twelve points. For Britain, Jack Kitchen headed the scorechart with 17 points as his side claimed a hard-fought 59-49 success. Reflecting, St.Austell were now without Chris Blewett and Lewis Philp. The former had to have a metal plate put in his arm just above the elbow joint for the bones to knit back together, while Philp's injuries were unfortunately to keep him out of action for good. Trevor Redmond found he had no alternative but to seek a suitable replacement, so he asked former Rye House junior Mike Keen to join him at St. Austell as reserve. Mike said, "My best early encouragement came from two people Trevor Redmond and Lew Coffin, finally I got a regular team place with Swindon in 1965."

When it was announced that Par Moor was to host the second Test match between Great Britain and the Overseas, speculation was rife about the selections for the home nation. Meanwhile, the Gulls had to make the arduous journey to Newcastle for a league match on 29 July. St. Austell gave a fine account of themselves, going down to the Diamonds by the smallest of margins. One thing that may have aided the visitors' morale was Brian Craven blowing his engine, meaning he ended up riding strange machinery all evening. Full result: Newcastle 40 (Ivan Mauger 12; Mike Watkin 7; Bob Duckworth 7; Craven 5; Peter Kelly 5; Jack Winstanley 3; Russ Dent 1) St. Austell 37 (Ray Cresp 9; Chris Julian 8; George Major 8; Glyn Chandler 6; Trevor Redmond 4; Mike Keen 2; Ray Wickett 0). After Newcastle had edged to victory, Cresp challenged Mauger for the Silver Sash and although the Aussie tried hard, it was the young Kiwi who retained the title.

Mauger again had the better of Cresp in the second half racing, when winning the Diamond Stakes final. George Major explained how he developed a friendship with Ivan Mauger. The two Majors of different spellings became travelling companions to various tracks around the country. George was still signed to his parent club Oxford where Ivan 'guested' on several occasions. Ivan then riding for Newcastle in the Provincial League enjoyed his guest rides for Oxford, where he often stayed at George's mother's house. George described the former World Champion as being extremely dedicated.

On 30 July, Cornish Stadium hosted a Provincial League match versus Stoke. The St. Austell side gave solid performance down the line and included a 5-point return from Ray Wickett, who each time came through from behind. Glyn Chandler was again in buoyant mood, having bagged another maximum. Turning to the Potters, only Colin Pratt and Ken Adams managed to score points against the home side. Ken Adams completed ten years for Stoke and was the club's highest scorer. Colin Pratt who came of age that season took his average to over ten. Full result: St. Austell 49 (Glyn Chandler 12; Ray Cresp 10; George Major 10; Trevor Redmond 6; Ray Wickett 5; Chris Julian 4;

Ron Bassett one of the St.Austell pushers 1949-1963 on track with Stoke riders.

Mike Keen 2) Stoke 29 (Pratt 9; Adams 7; Peter Jarman 4; Eric Hockaday 3; Kid Bodie 2; Ray Harris 2; Ron Sharp 2).

Glyn Chandler reminisced about the good friends he made at St. Austell. He often stayed with Chris Blewett when riding at Par Moor. He said Chris Julian often stayed with him when they were riding away. His comments reinforced Ray Wickett's thoughts about the Gulls' comradeship. Among many tales, there was a funny story about when they were once late for a meeting. George Major rang T.R., persuading him to run the second-half racing first so they could be there to ride. Major then drove the van at break neck speed, while Chandler changed in the back to save time. Glyn was 'stripped off' when the van pulled alongside a bus and all the occupants stared at him. Major thought the incident hilarious and simply couldn't stop laughing!

On 2 August, the St. Austell lads travelled to Wolverhampton on further league business. The match was a cracker and a credit to both teams, who worked hard to produce a result, with everything hinging on the last heat. It was imperative 'The Gulls' score a 4-2 to force a draw. George Major took the lead on the third lap and held on for the win, but he was not supported. Vitally filling the minor scoring positions were the home duo of Rick France and Tommy Sweetman. During the meeting Chris Julian had struggled on borrowed machinery and it was most unlike him to come in last on three occasions.

Full result: Wolverhampton 40 (Rick France 10; Maury Mattingly 10; Tom Sweetman 8; Dave Hemus 5; Peter Adams 3; James Bond 2; Cyril Francis 2) St. Austell 38 (Ray Cresp 11; George Major 8; Trevor Redmond 7; Ray Wickett 6; Glyn Chandler 3; Chris Julian 2; and Mike Keen 1).

Back at the Cornish Stadium on 6 August, the Gulls entertained Cradley Heath in a Provincial League encounter, with Reg Hawken drafted in at reserve to replace the missing Mike Keen. The powerhouse for the Heathens was Ivor Brown, who had a reputation for being a hard rider. Brown had his moment of glory at Par Moor in heats eight and nine, winning both in times of under 71.0 seconds. However, St. Austell again put in a good performance.

Glyn Chandler raced to another maximum, while Ray Cresp was back to his old form and also got twelve points on the scoresheet. In support 'full throttle man' Chris Julian roared to ten point's which was an especially pleasing result after he experienced several problems at Wolverhampton. Full result: St. Austell 47 (Chandler 12; Cresp 12; Julian 10; George Major 8; Trevor Redmond 3; Ray Wickett 2; Reg Hawken 0) Cradley Heath 31 (Brown 11; John Hart 7; John Edwards 4; Alan Totney 3; Ivor Davies 2; Harry Bastable 2; Derek Timms 2).

Two days later George Major made big news for Oxford by beating Peter Craven in a National League match. This feat occurred in heat thirteen, when the 'Pocket Rocket', with all his skill and track wizardry, couldn't pass the Cheetahs' reserve. Major's well earned 7 points helped secure a 45-33 win for Oxford over the Aces. George reflects on this later.

On Saturday 10 August, a Best Pairs meeting was run at Cradley Heath in which Glyn Chandler & George Major took part. The home fans saw Ivor Brown and his teammate Ivor 'Digger' Davies dash to victory on 27 points. Charlie Monk and Danny Dunton could not ride so their places were filled by, former 'Gull' Derek Timms and the bearded Jimmy Squibb.

They did well to total twenty points, with Squibb scoring sixteen of them. Meanwhile, the St. Austell pair of George Major and Glyn Chandler went well until Major fractured his frame. They would have probably finished as runners-up, but had to be satisfied with fourth spot in the end, Chandler scoring 12 points, whist Major tallied 6 points.

Regrettably, promoter Wally Mawdsley 'was put in between a rock and a hard place' when he announced the collapse of New Cross Speedway. This meant Jimmy Squibb moving to Exeter, Stan Stevens to Southampton and the other riders going to the Control Board for allocation. This was a worrying scenario for more than one South Coast club and could have been a death knell for others struggling to keep afloat.

Meanwhile, Glyn Chandler was doing a bit of coaching for the Weymouth Royals. He was helping Lew Coffin to supervise their practice session. TR was also busy behind the scenes trying to organize his winter tour. The date of 13 August may have been unlucky for some, but it wasn't for the spectators who witnessed a cracking night of racing at the Cornish Stadium as Britain and 'The Overseas' locked horns in Test match action. Bob Duckworth was a non-starter, so Colin McKee of Hackney and Middlesbrough's Kevin Torpie were drafted in to share his scheduled rides. Home riders Ray Cresp and Trevor Redmond collectively scooped 23 points.

Poole's Geoff Mudge came out on top of the scorechart with a total of thirteen. For those people who came to watch Ivan Mauger they weren't disappointed, as he netted 12 points. For Britain, George Major top scored with 13 points, while George Hunter hit a round dozen. Their efforts couldn't prevent the 'Overseas' side from snatching a 6-point success though. Full result: Britain 51 (Major 13; Hunter 12; Jimmy Squibb 9; Chris Julian 7; Glyn Chandler 5; Len Silver 5; Eric Martyn 0;) Les McGillivray (Res) DNR; Cliff Cox (Res) DNR) Overseas 57 (Geoff Mudge 13; Redmond 12; Ivan Mauger 12; Cresp 11; Charlie Monk 9; McKee 0; Torpie 0).

As shown Martyn failed to score for the home nation, but he knew when he agreed to fill in he wasn't going to be paid. Locally based, he worked for Eric Roberts until he was twenty years of age and often helped Chris Julian clean his gear on race nights at Par Moor. After the meeting the riders were treated to some warm Cornish hospitality kindly provided by Mrs. Bonney and Mrs.Pote. The two ladies spent all day cooking twenty chickens, while also making home made pasties, bread and cakes.

Ivan Mauger remembered riding at Cornish Stadium. He said, "Who could forget T.R. the promoter of St.Austell, such a larger than life character and a very proud New Zealander. I loved travelling to Cornwall in the days before the motorways. When we are in England at least once a year we still try to avoid the motorways as much as possible. We love going through the little villages.

Eric Martyn on parade at Par Moor.

Of course there were, and still are, times when we are in a hurry. Then the motorways are great." Ivan anticipated meeting his friend George Major at Coventry in March 2007 at the V.S.R.A. dinner.

Just three days later there was more speedway action at the Cornish Stadium with a Provincial League meeting against Newcastle. The encounter saw young Eric Martyn make his team debut for the Gulls in place of Reg Hawken at the reserve berth.

Under a black sky the spectators were there to cheer their local heroes, while also getting another glimpse of the new Diamonds' sensation Ivan Mauger.

Peter Goodman a former engineering colleague of the author, who now resides in Trelawney Road, St. Austell, remembered the Kiwi. He said: 'I was only a young lad at the time but I recall Mauger. He was good then, he could take your breath away, he was definitely a future World Champion!' Also in the Newcastle side was Peter Craven's brother Brian, who top-scored alongside Mauger, both hitting 12 points. The match was close, but bad weather put paid to any fast times.

After heat 8 the conditions deteriorated as the torrential rain beat down on the track, riders and spectators. Despite the conditions the meeting ran its course and by the final heat, St. Austell had a safety cushion and could still win even if the visitors registered maximum points. As it was, Chris Julian made a brilliant gate and was chased in vain by Mauger for four laps. The meeting had its memorable moments particularly the last heat. Years, later Julian and Mauger would be teamsters at Exeter.

Full result: St. Austell 42 (Ray Cresp 10; George Major 9; Chris Julian 8; Glyn Chandler 7; Trevor Redmond 5; Ray Wickett 3; Eric Martyn 0) The scores for Newcastle 36 (Craven 12; Mauger 12; Jack Winstanley 5; Mike Watkin 2; Peter Kelly 2; Bob Duckworth 2; Russ Dent 1). Understandably, the second half racing was abandoned due to the bad weather.

Eric Martyn recently explained a strange coincidence, which is worthy of a mention. He has a daughter who married a lad from Glasgow. When visiting Scotland to meet his son-in-law's family, he mentioned he had ridden speedway in the country. Lo and behold, his son-in-law's father Robert Carmichael, had been a pusher at the White City Stadium during that period!

On the same evening that the Gulls were defeating Newcastle, St. Austell rider Bob Warner appeared in a challenge match at Weymouth. He rode for a Southern Stars Select and bagged an impressive tally of 8 points. However, it was the home team who won 42-36, with Lew Coffin topping their scoring on 11 points.

Ray Cresp and Trevor Redmond rode for a Provincial League Select against Norwich at 'The Firs' on 17 August, and in atrocious conditions, both teams worked tirelessly to stay on their machines in an effort to produce some good racing. It was a close match, which the home side eventually won 40-38. Cresp scored 6 points for his side, while T.R. uncharacteristically failed to get off the mark. Heat one was a farce and shaped Redmond's evening. Jimmy Gooch fell on the first bend, with Terry Betts subsequently falling on the third turn. Redmond had no alternative than to lay down his machine to avoid the stricken rider, only to be excluded by the A.C.U. referee. He was gutted with the decision, but amazingly the meeting official changed his mind and allowed all four riders back for the re-run. Although given a reprieve, he still trailed in last. On the other side of the coin, home rider Olle Nygren revelled on the wet track and headed the Stars' scoring with eleven points. On the same night Jon Erskine who had rode for Neath and 'The Gulls' made his debut for Swindon. He rode in eleven meetings for 'The Robins'.

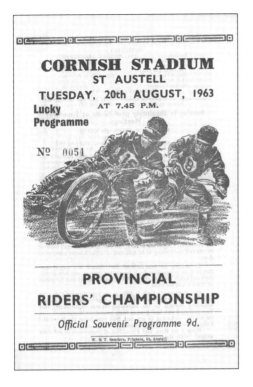

CORNISH STADIUM
ST AUSTELL
TUESDAY, 20th AUGUST, 1963
AT 7.45 P.M.
Lucky
Programme

Nº 0054

PROVINCIAL
RIDERS' CHAMPIONSHIP

Official Souvenir Programme 9d.

W. & T. Sanders, Printers, St. Austell

Programme for Riders Championship
20 August 1963.

St.Austell would have a good representation in the 1963 Provincial League Riders' Championship at Belle Vue on 28 September. Three riders, Ray Cresp, George Major and Trevor Redmond had all made it through to the prestigious Manchester final.

The St.Austell qualifying round was held on 20 August in front of a very good crowd. The two former Devils, Cliff Cox and Jimmy Squibb top scored with fourteen points each, with the former putting in two good times just over 70.0 seconds.

Meanwhile, top-flight Gulls' representative's Ray Cresp and George Major both registered 13-point tallies. The two went head-to-head in heat eighteen and literally raced wheel-to-wheel for four laps. On the very last bend, Major forced his front wheel ahead and went on to triumph by the slightest of margins. A little further down the field, Ray Wickett filled the boots of the missing Tim Bungay and rode extremely well to take a win, a second and two third places. His victory over Pete Munday and Tony Lewis in heat ten was particularly memorable. These are the full results: Squibb 14; Cox 14; Cresp 13; Major 13; Geoff Mudge 11; Chris Julian 10; T.Redmond 9; Ray Wickett 7; Norman Strachan 7; Glyn Chandler 4; Tony Lewis 4; Harry Edwards 4; Pete Munday 4;

Kevin Torpie 3; Stan Clark 3; Eric Martyn 0.

The following night, Ray Cresp top scored with George Hunter in the same competition at Hackney, both riders notching 14 points. Cresp's only defeat was at the hands of Hunter in heat three. Meanwhile, his St. Austell colleague George Major finished in equal sixth position on eight points. Fellow Gull Chris Julian appeared at Poole on the same evening, but he didn't fare as well, netting just six points in a meeting won by Poole favourite Ross Gilbertson, courtesy of a 15-point maximum.

As the competition progressed, Ray Cresp and Chris Julian found themselves riding at Dudley Wood on 24 August. Cresp again top scored with 13 points, sharing the top spot with Eric Boocock on that occasion. Lewis Philp was still in hospital and also on the minds of many people. The St. Austell Speedway Supporters' Club held a collection for him and his colleague Ray Wickett kindly donated his earnings to his injured friend, commenting: 'I was only too pleased to help.'

On 27 August, St. Austell were at home to Rayleigh in a Provincial League fixture. Some brilliant riding from Chris Julian, Ray Cresp, George Major and Glyn Chandler sealed the meeting and the Gulls were never really threatened.

In again at reserve was young Eric Martyn, who proved to local supporters that given time he could develop into a useful speedway rider. For the Rockets Stan Clark and former Gull Maurie McDermott proved the only useful opponents. Full result: St. Austell 48 (C.Julian 12; G.Major 11; R.Cresp 10; G.Chandler 9; T.Redmond 5; E.Martyn 1; R.Wickett 0) Rayleigh 30 (S.Clark 7; M.McDermott 7; L.McGillivray 6; H.Edwards 5; R.Bowers 3; S.McGillivray 1; P.McKenzie 1). In the second half, Cresp defeated Major in the West of England Match Race.

On 31 August, Trevor Redmond and Ray Cresp travelled to Stoke to participate in the Britain versus Overseas Test. Unfortunately, major traffic problems in Wolverhampton caused a few anxious moments prior to the match and star guest Pat Phoenix was slightly delayed in taking her seat. (Pat Phoenix was a television 'soap-star' of her era, who played Elsie Tanner in Coronation Street) Poole's Ross Gilbertson was also late for the tapes up. George Hunter rode well for Britain, coming from the back in heat five to pass Cresp and Geoff Mudge.

The Overseas' duo suffered a similar fate in heat eleven, when Jimmy Squibb and Pete Jarman did the same thing. Regrettably, Redmond had an off night,

The Gulls on parade, right to left, Chris Julian, George Major, Ray Cresp, Glyn Chandler and Eric Martyn.

mustering just three points. At the other end of the scales, it was Ivan Mauger who led the way for 'The Overseas' side with fifteen points. The Test was a credit to Stoke promoter Reg Fearman, who was duly rewarded with a huge crowd. Full result: Britain 72 (Colin Pratt 17; Squibb 14; Gilbertson 13; Hunter 12; Jarman 9; Ken Adams 7; Eric Hockaday 0) Overseas 36 (Mauger 15; Charlie Monk 8; Cresp 6; Mudge 3; Redmond 3; Bob Duckworth 1; Bluey Scott 0; Colin McKee 0).

On the same evening, Chris Julian appeared for London in the Festival Trophy at Edinburgh and 'The Monarchs' duly beat his side 48-30. Julian secured just a second and a third finishing on the night with a total of three points. The Scottish outfit proved too powerful for the quickly assembled select side.

In the Provincial League, St. Austell were now challenging rivals Exeter and holding a satisfactory mid-table position. The Gulls' programme continued on 3 September with a win over Hackney. It was highly entertaining match, with visitors Norman Hunter, Trevor Hedge and Jim Heard producing some amazing racing. Indeed, Hunter raced away with heat one to signify it wasn't going to be a push over. Cresp won easily in heat two and with Major coming in third. The home side moved marginally ahead. In heat six, Hunter came from behind to get between the fabulous pairing of Cresp and Major. Meanwhile, Hedge was equally as brilliant taking heats seven and thirteen. Full result: St. Austell 42 (Chris Julian 11; Glyn Chandler 10; Cresp 9; Major 9; Trevor Redmond 2; Ray Wickett 1; Eric Martyn 0) Hackney 36 (Hunter 12; Hedge 8; Heard 7; Colin McKee 3; Peter Sampson 3; Wal Morton 2; Malcolm Simmons 1).

The following evening, Ray Cresp rode for a Provincial League representative side versus a National League 'B' team at Hackney. Played out on a waterlogged track, he bagged thirteen points and helped his side to a 69-39 success. The only resistance from their opponents came from the spirited tiger-like riding of Cyril Maidment, who recorded 15 points from seven rides.

The speedway press continued to speculate over who was going to win the World Final at Wembley Stadium on 14 September. Would it be Barry Briggs, Ove Fundin, Peter Craven, Bjorn Knutsson or Ronnie Moore? A crowd of up to 70,000 was expected and tickets were on sale from the St. Austell Supporters' Club at prices ranging from 5 shillings to £1-1-0. For those who don't remember how it ended up, the big night resulted in a win for Ove Fundin, with Bjorn Knutsson in second place and Barry Briggs third.

Meanwhile, Trevor Redmond was back in Scotland to ride in a challenge match. This time he appeared for The Rest against a team simply labeled as Scots. Long Eaton's Charlie Monk looked the most impressive rider on the night. Charlie was beaten only once all evening, namely by Willie Templeton in the last heat. The final result was a 41-37 win for the Scots, with Redmond supplying seven points for his side.

On 10 September, the Gulls entertained Wolverhampton in a Provincial League match. Trevor Redmond had the knack and came back into form.

The high-scoring trio of Chris Julian, Ray Cresp and Glyn Chandler continued their good work. The only opposition from the Wolves came via Maury Mattingly.

Mattingly worked very hard all evening. Unfortunately, the rain again spoiled a good evening's racing, although it didn't prevent the homesters from taking victory by a decisive margin.

Full result: St. Austell 48 (Cresp 11; Chandler 10; Julian 10; George Major 8; Redmond 7; Eric Martyn 1; Ray Wickett 1) Wolverhampton 30 (Mattingly 12; Tommy Sweetman 5; Cyril Francis 4; James Bond 4; Ernie Baker 2; Dave Hemus 2; Rick France 1).

Trevor Redmond and Ray Cresp were again on Test match duty at Exeter on 16 September. This was a night for Britain to celebrate though, with Jimmy Squibb the toast of his side. He had settled to the County Ground raceway like a duck taking to water and despite a nasty looking tumble in one of his outings, still came back to record four race victories in his fourteen point tally. Alan Cowland was drafted in to help out the depleted 'Overseas side' and he did well, notching 11 points. Redmond gave a good account of himself in scoring 9 points, but Cresp had an off night, only managing a tally of 4. Full result: Britain 66 (Jim Squibb 14; Ross Gilbertson 13; Maury Mattingly 12; Len Silver 11; Cliff Cox 8; Doug Templeton 8) Overseas 42 (Geoff Mudge 13; Alan Cowland 11; Trevor Redmond 9; Ray Cresp 4; Bluey Scott 3; Bob Innocent 1; Ivan Mauger 1; George Summers 0).

The Gulls continued their good run at home by defeating Poole Pirates on 17 September. They were brilliantly lead by Trevor Redmond who bagged eleven points.

To be frank it could have been a bigger defeat for the Pirates than it actually was. Full result: St. Austell 45 (Redmond 11; George Major 10; Glyn Chandler 8; Chris Julian 8; Ray Cresp 5; Ray Wickett 5; Eric Martyn 1) Poole 33 (Ross Gilbertson 14; Geoff Mudge 10; Pete Munday 4; Tony Lewis 3; Norman Strachan 2; Tim Bungay 0; Pete Smith 0). In the second half, Ray Wickett won the 'Reserves Round-Up' from Smith, while Martyn was deserving of credit for keeping Strachan at the rear. Meanwhile, Cresp won the 'St.Blazey Scratch Race' and Redmond was victorious in 'The Big Four'.

Ken Tucker of Tresillian briefed the author Jerry about his love of speedway and how he supported relative Eric Martyn in the old days. He said, "I always tried to support local riders, I was so sad when our League Speedway finished. When the Claycountry Moto-Parc opened in 1997 my daughter Margaret and I enjoyed every match we attended. Whether it was the Gulls or the Trelawny Tigers we tried to be there. Sadly in 2006 Ken passed away, although missed by his family they have the reassurance that his life was that much richer for being a speedway fan, "Up the Gulls"

Potential League contenders St. Austell travelled to Hackney on 18 September, only to be met by a wet track. Regrettably, the circuit had been over-watered. The track was akin to a quagmire. Trevor Redmond could have refused to ride on it because of the safety issues, but he wasn't that sort of chap! As a result, the Gulls were all at sea, with most heats being decided at the gate. Full result: Hackney 54 (Norman Hunter 11; Colin McKee 10; Trevor Hedge 9; Pete Sampson 8; Malcolm Simmons 8; Jim Heard 7; David Crane 1) St. Austell 24 (Ray Cresp 8; Redmond 5; George Major 4; Glyn Chandler 3; Chris Julian 3; Bob Warner 1; Ray Wickett 0).

Ray Cresp did take the Scratch Race final in the second half, but it was of little consolation to the Gulls. A young Malcolm Simmons produced the talking point of the evening with a sensational ride from the back to pass both Cresp and Major. George Major had to settle for second spot behind Norman Hunter. Some think 'Cornish Gulls' have webbed feet but they couldn't cope with the apalling wet conditions!

On 21 September, Ray Cresp was invited to ride for Parker's Team in a challenge match at Belle Vue. The track was poorly prepared and the racing was generally dreary, with Cresp managing only 5 points. Despite his lowly contribution, his side still tasted victory, winning 49-31.

The Gulls completed their league fixtures with an easy win over Long Eaton at Par Moor on 24 September. As in the previous week's home match, St. Austell's big four of Chris Julian, Ray Cresp, Glyn Chandler and George Major did the bulk of the scoring. Julian was the pick of the bunch, showing cracking form to record another maximum, whilst Chandler dropped just a solitary point to Charlie Monk in the opening heat. Trevor Redmond suffered bad luck in the same race when his conrod went through the crankcase of his engine with a clatter and a puff of smoke, meaning he had to complete the meeting on borrowed machinery. Full result: St. Austell 49 (Julian 12; Chandler 11; Cresp 10; Major 9; Redmond 5; Ray Wickett 1; Eric Martyn 1) Long Eaton 29 (Monk 9; Bluey Scott 7; Ken Vale 6; Norman Storer 3; Slant Payling 2; Des Lukehurst 1; Geoff Penniket 1).

Unfortunately, the sad news reached Cornwall during the same evening that Peter Craven had died at the age of twenty-nine, having sustained serious injuries in a racing accident at Edinburgh the previous Friday. 'Peter was one of the greatest riders of all time', said Sheffield manager Frank Varey, 'I've seen them all since 1928 and to me there was no greater rider, I could watch him go around for hours.' Eric Boocock who was a guest rider for Edinburgh on that fateful night had this to say, "The loss of Peter Craven was a massive blow to British Speedway and it came at a time when the sport was in turmoil." The story of this wonderful ambassador for motor-sport is told in Brian Burford's book 'The Wizard of Balance'.

On 25 September, Ray Cresp was back in London to ride for the Overseas in a challenge match at Hackney. The Aussie contributed 6 points as his side went down to a narrow 41-37 defeat. The best race of the evening occurred in heat ten, when Alan Cowland and Ivan Mauger enjoyed a terrific tussle. Mauger missed the gate, while Cowland hit the front. The action had everyone spellbound. The Kiwi pushed hard and passed Cowland on the outside on the top bend. Coming into the home straight, however, Mauger's machine petered out, leaving Cowland to take the win.

The following evening, St. Austell rider George Major appeared in the Double Diamond Trophy event at Oxford. Nigel Boocock(Eric's brother)won the event with 14 points, but Major didn't fare too well, tallying just three.

The Provincial League Riders' Final was held at Hyde Road, Belle Vue on 28 September. Just imagine making the journey to Manchester on poor roads! All West Country eyes were on riders Ray Cresp (St. Austell), George Major (St. Austell), Trevor Redmond (St. Austell), Cliff Cox (Exeter), and Jimmy Squibb (Exeter). Also Ross Gilbertson and Geoff Mudge of Poole were in the thoughts of Pirate's fans.

George Major's first ride was in heat four, when he was up against Jack Kitchen, Maury Mattingly and Gilbertson. Needless to say they finished in that order, with George Major bringing up the rear. Heat five saw Ray Cresp have a brilliant 'gate', Ivor Brown chased but the overtake move didn't happen. Geoff Mudge was third and T.R. was unplaced. Apparently Cresp and Redmond had a rare old barney part way through the meeting. The fearless Cresp goaded Redmond by saying, "You mean promoters get 100,000 spectators here and we get thirty bob a point."(£1-50) Trevor retorted, "Ar, 'tis terrible I've got to ride and put my winnings in the hat to pay you!" Seriously though Trevor apologized to Ray for clanging him with his elbow because he had 'ace clanger' Ivor Brown hustling on the inside.

Heat seven saw Cresp demoted to third place behind Jack Kitchen and Ivan Mauger, who were both in good form and definitely the men to beat. Heat nine was a sight to behold, with Squibb producing an excellent effort to win from Colin Pratt, with Major in third spot. Heat twelve got Redmond off the mark, although he only managed third place. In heat fifteen, Cresp didn't make the gate, but Gilbertson was away. Rick France tried to split the pair, only to fall. After remounting, he gave chase only to be denied victory by an engine failure! In the next heat, Kitchen chalked up another win ahead of Cox, with T.R. in third position.

In Heat twenty-two Cresp and Major were pitched together against John Hart and Ken Adams. The dark horse Cresp hit the front and never looked back, while his teammate, Major, filled second place ahead of Adams. Heat twenty-four saw Trevor Redmond only take another third place and he was clearly aware that it wasn't good enough. Jack Kitchen and Ivan Mauger were through to the final, but what about the others? Maurie Mattingly, Clive Featherby, 'Crespie', Boocock and George Hunter had all finished on the nine-point mark. Ray Cresp who had been paid £5 start money was in the running for the £40 first prize money plus £1-10-0. per point(£1-50). Who could have guessed a sit down strike was about to occur? The rules stated that heat wins would decide this kind of situation, or failing that, fastest times. However, the riders were not happy and protested by sitting on the track. The officials relented and a five-man run off was decided. Many St.Austell fans thought Ray Cresp should be in the final so at least it appeased them! Hunter gated superbly, while behind there was bunching into the first bend, before Gilbertson edged ahead of Cresp and that's the way it finished.

The spectators loved this highly competitive racing, with one heard to comment: 'It's better than a World Final.' The final drew nigh as Kitchen, Mauger, Hunter and Gilbertson rolled up to the tapes. All four riders were under thirty and both Hunter and Mauger were under twenty-five years of age. George Hunter initially took the lead, but his moment of glory was short-lived. His motor coughed and spluttered, before he came to a halt. Mauger took up the lead and went on to win comfortably from Kitchen, while Gilbertson came in third. Mauger was subsequently crowned Champion with the usual laurels and presented with the trophy.

The speedway press was full of tributes to the late Peter Craven. From well-known journalists like Eric Linden, to ordinary speedway fans the tributes poured in at this time. The supporters at Par Moor would never forget the amazing riding of Craven, who was known as the 'Mighty Atom'.

George Major summed up his thoughts about Craven, who he had beaten on the odd occasion. Apparently someone asked Craven where his world championship bike was, and he quickly replied, "This is it". George said, "Peter Craven got on a bike and rode with every effort. He deserved his World Final win because he did it on a J.A.P. Many smaller riders like Peter Collins and Trevor Hedge did well with the two valve Jawa but Craven made riding a J.A.P. look easy when it wasn't. In my opinion it is fitting the Craven Shield was run to remember such a great rider."

George explained he was a big fan of the J.A.P. motor. He said, "The J.A.P. was a great engine, I think it was highly competitive in it's day. I couldn't get on with the Jawa when they came in from mainland Europe."

Even years later when George was riding at Birmingham he was still riding his steadfast J.A.P. Luckily the cutting of the story of George Major beating Peter Craven survived in peculiar circumstances. George lent journalist Peter Arnold some of his valuable speedway books, sadly Peter was killed in an accident and his precious books were never returned. Strangely, one of the speedway book's which Peter didn't take was lent to his nephew Kevin, the cutting of George's victory over P.C. was folded inside that edition.

The Sunday Express at the time punched out a hard-hitting headline, which stated: 'Rocket for Southampton as gates slump'. It appeared gates were 25 per cent down on the previous season and promoter Charlie Knott was indeed worried about the decline in attendances. He said: "We are concerned the team haven't pulled their weight and interest is waning, we don't want to be forced to close down." Unfortunately that is exactly what happened.

Speedway supporter Dave Collins, who was then serving in the R.A.F. in the Middle East, was stunned to hear his beloved Banister Court was to close. He said: "The Saints had a colourful history and I was pleased to have seen my Uncle Vic participate for them. I spent some time in the pits with Johnny Fitzpatrick and got to know many of the riders. What with Erskine Staride machines and Maury Mattingly frames being built just up the road from one another, Southampton was a great place to be in the 1950s." He concluded: 'The 1960s boasted riders such as Bjorn Knutsson and Barry Briggs; then it was gone. However, we were left with nostalgic memories!'

Incidentally, David Collins went on to be the press officer for the 'The B.W.O.C. St.Austell Gulls' in 1997. Today Dave still has a keen interest in speedway despite not being in the best of health.

The season finished at Par Moor on 1 October, when a challenge match pitched Cornwall against Devon. The Cornwall team was largely made up of St. Austell riders and similarly, the Devon side consisted mainly of the Exeter lads. Chris Julian raced to a faultless maximum.

Chris was showing he was one of the brightest prospects in speedway at the time. As usual, he received sound support from 'Crespie' and George Major as Cornwall swept to victory. The match was well attended, despite being hit by more inclement weather. It had been a poor season, with no less than eighteen meetings being affected by showers or rain. Trevor Redmond certainly missed a sales opportunity in not selling umbrellas!

The full result was: Cornwall 33 (Julian 12; Cresp 10; Major 8; Glyn Chandler 2; Eric Martyn 1) Devon 21 (Jimmy Squibb 7; Ray Wickett 6; Alan Cowland 4; Cliff Cox 2; Pat Flanagan 2). The after-meeting festivities continued for the riders who ate a hearty dinner, followed by drinks and dancing at Carlyon Bay. The thriving supporters club also invited the Exeter riders. The Carlyon Bay complex became home to the Cornwall Coliseum for many years before being demolished to make way for new waterside apartments. In 2002 developers Ampersand acquired the site with planning permission to build 511 holiday apartments and houses. None have been built yet due to problems with the sea defences.

The season was heralded a success despite the wet summer. In the Provincial League, the Gulls finished in a fully deserved third position. As such, it was a very bitter pill to swallow for genuine speedway fans when Trevor Redmond announced he was forming a partnership with Ian Hoskins and moving to White City, Glasgow.

It was indeed hard to comprehend for not only had St. Austell seen the last of its solo speedway, but the death knell had rung at Southampton's Banister Court home too!

On 4 October, Trevor Redmond and Ray Cresp again rode for the Overseas in a Test match at Wolverhampton. For T.R. it was a poor evening as he made no contribution to his side's score, but Cresp worked tirelessly to notch eight points. Ray was not only a 'good gater' but a fighter! His main disappointment of the evening came in heat twelve, when he and partner Bluey Scott looked certain for a 5-1, but were picked off by Ross Gilbertson and then Jimmy Squibb as Britain moved into a 10-point lead. Steadily, they built up their advantage thereafter to emerge comfortable winners. Full result: Britain 63 points (Jim Squibb 15; Ivor Brown 14; George Hunter 12; Ross Gilbertson 8; Tommy Sweetman 7; Pete Jarman 5; Dave Hemus 2; Harry Bastable 0) Overseas 45 points (Charlie Monk 13; Peter Vandenberg 12; Bob Duckworth 8; Ray Cresp 8; Bluey Scott 3; Colin McKee 1; Trevor Redmond 0; Cyril Francis 0).

The following evening, Trevor Redmond appeared in the Scottish Open Championship at Edinburgh. Unfortunately, he was never in contention and could only manage four points. At the other end of the scale Maury Mattingly easily secured the title, courtesy of a brilliant five-ride maximum.

A 'Best Pairs' Championship took place at Exeter's County Ground on 14 October, when George Major was fortunately on hand to fill a vacant spot, accompanying Cliff Cox. The eventual victors were Len Silver and Jimmy Squibb with a combined total of 19 points. Full result: Silver (11) and Squibb (8) = 19;

113

Chris Julian with that familiar broad grin we all knew and loved.

Ross Gilbertson (15) and Norman Strachan (2) = 17; Cox (11) and Major (4) = 15; Alan Cowland (11) and Des Lukehurst (4) = 15; Maury Mattingly (13) and Dennis Day (1) = 14; Maury McDermott (7) and George Summers (3) = 10.

For those who love statistics, here is a run through of who did what in 1963 for St. Austell. The side's top scorer was Fraddon's Chris Julian, who bagged 224 points from twenty-seven matches. Chris was the worthy winner of the St.Austell Supporters Club trophy. George Major did well too, especially when he discovered the big cam in June. Ray Cresp was indeed an asset, proving a brilliant partner for Major, and the author said he can dismiss the lie that he was sacked by Ipswich.

Ray Cresp will go down as one of the fastest riders from the gate of all time, along with Peter Moore, Jack Biggs, Bob Kilby, Ryan Sullivan and Jason Crump. Going back to the riders who represented the Gulls, Trevor Redmond fell from being a ten point man with Neath to a second string! However, it mustn't be forgotten that he had served his apprenticeship on track riding at Aldershot then moved to Wembley, Bradford, Bristol, Wolverhampton and Neath, before juggling all the hats at St.Austell. Chris Blewett started well until he broke his arm at Exeter, which was an injury that unfortunately finished his season.

The 1963 Statistical summary:

	Matches	Points	Bonus	Total
Chris Julian	27	222	2	224
George Major	27	186	29	215
Ray Cresp	24	195	13	208
Glyn Chandler	27	195	11	206
Trevor Redmond	27	181	25	206
Ray Wickett	26	52	11	63
Bob Warner	12	26	6	32
Chris Blewett	5	27	4	31
Mike Keen	3	5	1	6
Fred Powell	3	3	1	4
Eric Martyn	6	4	0	4
Lewis Philp	1	0	0	0
Reg Hawken	1	0	0	0
Ray Harkiss	1	0	0	0

1964
The riders move to other clubs

Picking over the bones of the 1963 season, here are the high and low points! The best home result was a 58-19 success against Edinburgh. The worst home result was a 41-37 reverse at the hands of Sheffield. The best away result was a 44-34 victory at Rayleigh, while the worst performance was a hefty 54-24 defeat at Hackney.

Despite the success of 1963, Trevor Redmond still moved to Glasgow in 1964. T.R. joked that he now had a telephone in the office, but only Ian Hoskins truly knows what lured him north of the Border. Trevor's name was linked with businessman Doug Ellis, who became the Aston Villa Chairman. It was thought he was Trevor's financial partner. Trevor rode regularly for Glasgow in 1964 where he scored 144 League points for the club. In 1965 something was said which was the cue for the Kiwi to finally hang up his leathers, although Trevor Redmond did pull them on again a few times, but only for demonstration purposes.

The problem of running Cornish speedway had been there even a decade before. The financial burden of travelling costs made Cornwall geographically handicapped and Redmond found he was losing money on the gates week after week. Never forget he was a brilliant team-man in speedway, but also an astute businessman. One can only speculate that had T.R. enjoyed the same kind of gates as the Luke family had in the early 1950s, then maybe the Gulls would have continued. Although Redmond continued his involvement in speedway, his only interest at Par Moor from this point on was stock car and banger racing, which continued into the 1980s. He also promoted stock car racing at Newton Abbot.

The summer of 1964 saw Cornish Grass-track racing flourish. The British Sporting Sidecar Association held meetings at Hayle and at the mountain circuit at Portreath. More often than not Phil Williams battled with Bill Uren for sidecar honors. Meanwhile Adrian Kessell and Chris Julian topped the solo events. The former not only excelled in Cornwall, but won in the Southern Centre, South West Centre and the Wessex Centre.

In 1964 when Trevor Redmond moved to Glasgow, it was the year the leagues split so George Major decided to stay with the A.C.U. and returned to Oxford. Just before the start of the season T.R. called into George's workshop one day totally out of the blue. He said he was on his way to Glasgow and wondered if Major had changed his mind and would sign again for him. T.R. said George would sometimes be able to fly up to Scotland. George was not too keen on flying, and had this vision in his head of Trevor dressed in a leather helmet and goggles at the controls of a 'Tiger Moth.' As George walked out into the yard to see his guest off he was amazed to see T.R. was driving a brand new car. George recollects it was a Morris 1100. Trevor had removed the back seat to put in a bike, with the wheels out. The other machine was shoved in the back with the wheel hanging out and the boot lid tied down. George 'couldn't believe his eyes.' T.R. said, "Well I've gotta get 'em up there". He laughed heartily and drove off. George reminisced that whilst at Oxford he built up a friendship with John Hart. The two became teamsters and travelling companions. George explained, "Although I didn't ride for Trevor again, I did return to ride back in the Provincial League out of loyalty to the A.C.U."

He continued, "The First Division promoters were not rewarded in any way, we were just used to make up the numbers. So by Whitsun I had signed for Cradley Heath where I had far and away my best season to date. Rounding off the racing season I qualified to represent my club in the Provincial League Riders Final but a crash at Newport the night before put paid to that. I broke my wrist. The following year saw the amalgamation of the leagues to form the British League. I stayed with Cradley Heath and although at First Division level and ravaged by injuries I still maintained a reasonable average."

John Hart rode at Cradley with George and yet again they were to be in the same team. In 1966 George was moved by 'Rider Control' to Sheffield to link with John again. George broke his femur, commonly known as the 'thigh bone', whilst riding at Sheffield, which kept him of action for the best part of a year. George returned to the side as a reserve while John topped the averages. George stayed at First Division level riding for Leicester where he partnered Anders Michenek. When George lost his team place he returned to Oxford where he remained until 1970. At the Monmore Green track, George Major made the acquaintence of Howard Cole and his son-in-law Jim Bond, who became a

Pit Marshall Ron Bassett chats to George Major at Claycountry Moto-Parc when the Isle of Wight were visitors. George donned his leathers and did a demonstration ride to show he hasn't lost any of his racing edge. Photo John Yeo.

great J.A.P. engine specialist.

George continued, "Due to a dispute with the promoter at Oxford outside the sport, he dropped me half way through the season. After a short lay-off I agreed to help Joe Thurley at Doncaster, who were riding in the second division." At Doncaster George became the lynchpin of the team with Gordon McGregor as the lead off man in shiny black leathers. Gordon was a canny Scot who had a vast knowledge of bikes and engines. George continued, "The following year Joe Thurley switched to Birmingham so I decided to stay with him and remained there for five seasons. I was privileged to captain the most successful 'Brummies' side to two League Championships and a Cup double. Joe's decision not to include me in his 1976 First Division side was disappointing. To leave me out was a blow, but I received a few offers from other tracks. I decided to wait and see. However, by then my haulage business was taking more and more time, so my speedway career ended without me really making a conscious decision to step down." George Major in later years became involved with speedway management. George managed the Isle of Wight Premier League side. Sadly he is no longer involved in speedway coaching.

Ivor Toms pictured in 1994 with the J.A.P. he restored, originally owned by speedway ace Charlie Monk. Inset Ivor in his racing days, J & S Publications.

Trevor Redmond's sense of humour was always witty, but he could be dry. Mike Williams of Park Way, St. Austell, a banger-racing competitor, recently told the story of his first encounter with T.R. He said:'It was my first meeting, I was a bit nervous, but I enjoyed myself. Unfortunately my car rolled over and it caught fire.' 'Trevor came round to us all at the end of the meeting and handed us our start money, he said "thanks for coming, but don't come again because you cost me the price of a fire extinguisher", he didn't mean it of course.' To-day, Mike Williams continues in car racing competition, driving 'Bangers' and 'Reliants'.

Meanwhile, the winter of 1963 took some of the St. Austell team members to sunnier climes to continue riding. The others returned to their daily occupations and it was business as usual. There were quite a number of the West Country riders who were involved in the motor trade, including Brian Crutcher, Ivor Toms, Lewis Philp, Francis Cann and Len Silver to name just a few.

Sidecar speedway continued alongside car racing at Par Moor in 1964 and this will be examined a little more closely in the next chapter. It is fair to comment that the competitive edge to the racing from this point on was not as

Left: Chris in the pits at Cradley.

Below: Chris Julian having some assistance by Cradley Heath teamster Roy Trigg.

Oppsite page: Chris Julian in action for Cradley(second right) photo J & S Publications.

fierce, because the racing became basically of a demonstration nature rather than being under the auspices of the Auto-Cycle Union. Needless to say the participants enjoyed themselves immensely; if they didn't it would have petered out for good.

The year also saw the Gulls' team scatter to the four winds. Some continued riding, while others retired from the sport. Chris Julian moved to Glasgow with Trevor Redmond and went from strength to strength. Chris sustained a serious injury at Sheffield but returned to form before the end of the season, so much so in fact that he represented Scotland in the Test matches against England. With the Monarch's Willie Templeton, Chris Julian won the Scottish Best Pairs. A year later, in 1965, he made his debut at Swindon but only rode a handful of meetings. In the same year Chris again met up with George Major and Glyn Chandler, joining them at Cradley Heath. Chris Julian also represented Cornwall in the Inter Centre Grass-track team. Despite an un-orthodox style Chris went on to be a steady point's scorer on track and rode for Newport before transferring to Exeter where he won a League Winners medal in 1974. He rode for a while at Mildenhall and Weymouth before finally hanging up his leathers after 19 years.

Away from speedway Chris Julian enjoyed building and flying gyrocopters. Unfortunately, Chris lost his life in a flying accident at R.A.F. Kemble in 1997,

Eric Martyn(right) presenting the book launch of St.Austell Speedway The Early Years at Trewoon Village Hall in 2006 with Jeremy Jackson(left) and veteran Alf Webster(centre), photo Colin Rugg.

a week before the re-birth of speedway at Claycounty Moto-Parc near Nanpean. The author spent many a happy hour in Chris' company at his workshop at Higher Fraddon and concludes he had so much presence, spirit and life he could fill Wembley Stadium. Speedway enthusiast Roger Beaman from Oldbury summed up Chris as 'One of the great Cradley riders to wear the green and white because he was one of the greatest triers at the Dudley Wood track.'

The other Chris, the adopted Cornishman Chris Blewett moved to Exeter. The night Chris Blewett beat Barry Briggs at the County Ground is still a talking point today, particularly now Chris has passed away. Ray Wickett however had a few rides for Glasgow before he too linked with Exeter.

Ray's best riding years were probably at Exeter and West Ham. His favourite tracks were Owlerton and Old Meadowbank. Ray was indeed another great character who was a test rider for B.S.A. Motorcycles in Birmingham. He also did some amazing stunts on bikes including riding through tunnels of fire. He may not have been a world champion but his life was so much richer for having 'ridden on the shale'. Ray who lived at Stratton remained in touch with many of the old 'Gulls' until his untimely passing after several years of ill health.

Ivor Toms didn't return to 'solo' speedway, while Eric Martyn, who was then beginning to bloom as a good speedway rider, retired from motor-sport for a short period before taking up scrambling. Eric, who was born at Helston grew up at a hamlet called Kestle near Mevagissey, before working for lifelong friend Eric Roberts.

For many years Eric worked for Associated Asphalt a subsidary company of china clay giant English China Clays. For much of his life, Eric has worked tirelessly for the Cornwall A.C.U.Centre. He has filled many positions and is the current President of the Centre. It is important to recognise he is also an honorary life member. Eric was a regular presenter when the Gulls returned to action at the Claycountry Moto Parc in 1997, since then he has retained an active interest in following his beloved speedway particularly the fortunes on track of Elite League rider Chris 'Bomber' Harris who also hails from Cornwall. Today Eric Martyn's occupation as a training manager takes him all over the country. Many describe Eric who is in his sixties as a busy person but I think a human dynamo fits the bill absolutely.

Glyn Chandler went on to ride for Long Eaton where he had a few maximums. He even captained the side a few times. He had a few more outings at Oxford and Cradley Heath before retiring. His biking days were not yet over because in 1973 Glyn rode in the Isle of Man Tourist Trophy Races as Dennis Keen's sidecar partner. Following this he got the speedway bug again and turned out for demonstration races at home and abroad. He has rode in many competitions including Briggo's Golden Greats and the Speedway Classic Championship. Today, Glyn and his wife Sally enjoy riding his classic motorcycles on the island of Alderney.

Mike Keen who only rode in a handful of meeting's in a 'Gulls' jacket signed for Oxford for a £50 fee. He had to compete for a team place with Eddie Reeves but finally got his break with Swindon Robins. In 1965 the little lad with the wicked smile and big heart excelled after some equipment changes advised by maestro Barry Briggs. Mike went on to make 228 appearances for his club bagging a total of 1305 points, which was an amazing achievement.

Some have asked the author to mention 'Football at Cornish Stadium' beside the A390. In later years the home team to play at the stadium were the 'Heavy Transport' side. Heavy Transport were a subsidary of E.C.C. whose workshops and lorry park were just across the road from the stadium. The side continued to play there until tarmacadam was laid across part of the pitch. Probably the

Reunited in grief for a former speedway friend, Lewis Philp. (From right to left) Chris Julian, Ivor Toms(teamsters St. Austell and Plymouth)Ken Westaway(sidecar ace) Ron Bassett (trackstaff 50/60s) Trevor Redmond (rider and promoter) Chris Blewett (teamster) Bill Dalley(track announcer) Ray Wickett(teamster and life long friend)

most famous name to play at Par Moor was Nigel Martyn. He turned out there as a teenager with his brother. Nigel who was from Bethel went on to be the Everton goalkeeper and was capped for England many times. Although mainly the No.2 goalie for his country, many claim he should have been the number one choice. Nigel has since hung up his playing boots! Today the old work-shops and lorry-park have been turned into a multi purpose business park.

Lawrence Stephens a speedway fan for more years than he can remember summed up his feelings about the 'good old days' of Cornish Stadium. He said, "I felt privileged to have seen so many great riders over the years. I was lucky in the sense I have known the Westaway brothers, who competed in sidecar events from when they were very young. I also got to know several other local riders and had the bonus of knowing people like the late Harold Bull, a fifties 'Gull' and a good friend. When I worked for Heavy Transport I passed the stadium everyday. Sadly it's gone and I fear we will never see the crowds or the enthusi-asm for the sport here again in the Duchy."

Here we remember the year 1964 with a montage of national and local sporting advertisements.

1959-86
The sidecar years

In 1959, a new form of high-octane action hit the Par Moor track on a regular basis, namely sidecar speedway. Following a tour by the Australians, Jim Davies and Peter Speering, the seeds were sown in Britain. Sidecar racing had been around since 1928 when speedway spread like wildfire across the UK, but it had failed to catch on in like it had in Australia.

Two main groups enjoyed the three-wheeled action here in Britain, one in the Midlands and the other in Cornwall. The 'pioneers' in the Duchy were Roy Wedlake of St.Austell, Phil Williams of Tywardreath, and Pat Crawford of Saltash. Meanwhile, in the Midlands, the sidecar aces were Bill Evans, Vic Artus, Ian Paskin, Harold Hill, Ivor Lawrence and Jeff Lucy. In both areas, many more followed their tyre tracks.

The man who was instrumental in getting sidecar speedway started at Par Moor was Roy Wedlake, who was indeed a character. Unfortunately, he passed away a number of years ago and is still very much missed. Trevor Redmond once mailed Roy from Australia addressing it to R.Wedlake, St.Austell, Cornwall, England and believe it or not it found its destination. The tales about him are legendary and the one about him riding the length of Par Harbor with the sidecar wheel hanging over the quay wall is often still repeated. In local trials events he rode with friend Roy Vincent.

Roy Wedlake was an able man with tools in his hand and he helped a few riders, even at big venues like Wembley. He was a competent vehicle mechanic, who was a specialist on Ford cars, but he dabbled in many other occupations from window cleaning to selling wood. The wood yard at the end of Carclaze Road where Roy did his 'logging' was flattened to make way for the car park, which was completed for the Queen's Silver Jubilee in 1977. There are also tales of the outfit with the ladders. Roy had a successful 'window cleaning round' which involved some big contracts including the Lawn School, off Truro Road. Many years later he worked for Heavy Transport at their workshops at Par Moor Road.

Roy Wedlake in his youth, photo W.Avery.

Back in the garage Roy was excellent at reconditioning cylinder heads where he used his own specialised cutting equipment. Many remark to this day at his expertise in this area. As for his car driving, he was rated more highly than Paddy Hopkirk, the rally driver, particulary bringing the darts team home from the Kings Arms at Luxulyan in his Vauxhall Cresta. Roy's antics on a sidecar outfit were well known to the local constabulary but one has to remember this was a different era of policing. There were two main factors, a warning from a policeman meant just that, and if you could outpace a Ford Anglia Panda car you got away with it!

Keith George who today lives at Lanjeth has a few boyhood memories of Roy Wedlake. He said, "Many a time Roy would stop his outfit at the bottom of Buckey Hill and shout across 'Do you want a lift?' I climbed aboard on what was just a board on the sidecar, I clung on for dear life as he flew up the hill with a cacophony of sound from the engine. On race day Roy would be over in the wood yard tuning up his bike which could be heard way down Slades Road, even at Avery's Motorcycles." Today old Buckey Hill has been closed due to a major road improvement and new housing.

Roy participates in the End to End Trial.

On 3 September 1959 Roy Wedlake, Ivor Toms and Chris Julian rode in the sidecar racing events at the Pennycross Stadium in Plymouth. Ken McKinlay's Lions took on Briggo's Overseas side. Speedway stars Ronnie Moore and Neil Street even drove karts! Paul Eustace has produced an excellent book about Plymouth Speedway with some rare photographs for anyone who is interested.

Roy Wedlake developed a deep and lasting friendship with George Newton, the former New Cross and Fleetwood leg trailer, who visited Roy and family at his home in Carclaze years after speedway had ceased. Andrew Wedlake, Roy's son marvelled at how Reg Hawken, his Dad's passenger clung onto the speedway outfit at speed. He said, "I had a go as a passenger for Ken Westaway in a demonstration at The British Bike Show for two laps around the Falmouth Recreation Ground some years ago. I was literally shaking when I got off. How Dad would have loved to have been part of it all on that particular day!"

Andy had his own successes in Cornish Grass-tracks. In the eighties and nineties he rode against some tough competitors such as Mark Rowe, Steve Jacobs, Michael Johns and Andy Robins. Andy used a variety of frames from Dula, Antig and Hagon. He said, "Dad and I usually argued over something

Wedlake leads at Pennycross Stadium, Plymouth.

about the bike!" Andy proved an asset to Cornwall in the National Centre Championships. Andy said, "Dennis Huddy was our team-manager and he did a good job trying to sort out all the arrangements. On the wider grass-track scene I rode in many of the bigger events in the Midlands, Wiltshire, Kent and Hampshire. My favourite rider of all time has to be the late Simon Wigg, I was so proud to race on the same grass-track circuit with such a legend. He was my Champion of Champions, such a brilliant rider."

Roy's love of Boxer dogs was well known locally and this gave an edge to his character. Jerry, the author, spotted this at the workshop in the late seventies. He said, "The bond between dog and master was there for all to see as the animal put his paws over the railings, Roy would quip "I'll smash you face in" but the love was definitely mutual. Roy explained that Boxers are loyal, good with children and have such good temperament.

After Phil Williams had introduced sidecar speedway racing to Ken Westaway of Carclaze Garage, St. Austell, he became very involved in the sport and continues to demonstrate the Aussie banked outfits to this day. Ken served his engineering apprenticeship at Heavy Transport on Par Moor Road and contin-

Ken Westaway and Andy Wedlake demonstrating the Aussie banked outfit at the British Bike Show at Falmouth, photo thanks Andy Wedlake

ued working there into his twenties. One night after work he met up with Williams, and without any persuasion he took his first ride on a speedway outfit. As they say, the rest is history.

Ken left his job at Heavy Transport to start his own business. As Ken was held in high esteem by management he was called into the office. The senior manager at that time, Len Matthews asked Ken why he was leaving and pleaded with him to stay. Ken's mind was made up and 'he went on his own'. One of Ken Westaway's favourite racing moments occurred at Par Moor in the 1960s. He was riding against his brother David, as well as Pat Crawford, Roy Wedlake, Phil Williams, Fred Tarr and Gerald Stoneman in a Handicap race. The seven outfits were staggered around the 360-yard track and although Westaway was half-a-lap behind the first man, he still fought his way to the front to take the chequered flag in front of a good crowd. Due to the problems created by riding at a stock-car track, which wasn't run under the auspices of the A.C.U., many of the riders bent the rulebook by the use of pseudonyms. Hence, there were names appearing like Ken West, Dave West and Phil Silvers to name a few. This in turn allowed the competitors to race in A.C.U. events at weekends using their own name.

Andy Wedlake in action at a local grass-track event riding a 500cc Antig, thanks J.Wedlake

Sidecar action at Par Moor,note the cobbled together riding gear, photo D.Stallworthy

Many of the Cornish aces rode at other stadiums including Mendip Raceway, Bristol, Exeter's County Ground and the Empire Stadium, Wembley. Indeed, Westaway's throttle cable broke during an event at Wembley and he ended up on the hallowed turf, much to the disgust of the steward. Not many riders from Cornwall can say they rode under the old Wembley 'twin towers'. Ken Westaway told another amusing story about his brother Dave. He said, "Dave always liked to get to meetings early so he left Cornwall to race at Mendip Raceway four hours before me. As we approached the circuit Dave was coming from the other direction, we couldn't believe it, I don't think Dave ever bought a map in his life!"

Ken Westaway was a good all-rounder and will be remembered for his road racing and sidecar grass-track, not to mention his successes in Pre-75 sidecar grass-track racing. Ken took several wins in the Southern Centre Grass-tracks against many of their established riders. In 1989 and 1990, he participated in the Past Master grass-track events held near Salisbury, Wiltshire. In 1995 he won the one day Golden Valley Club Pre 75 Grass-track event, the Cornish Sidecar Pre 75 title and the South West Pre 75 Sidecar title. Over the years Ken has helped many clubs including being the President of the Par 90 Grass-track club and a founder member of the White Gold Classic and Custom Bike Show Committee which ran successive fund-raisers in the nineties. He even rode the B.B.C. owned paramedic bike from the 'Casualty' programme from Bristol to Cornwall and returned it, all in his own time in the name of charity. For many years Ken was an active member of the Norton Owners Club.

In recent years, he has given help to his two racing son's Justin and Wayne, but more importantly he has shown his skilful tenacity with mechanical assistance to several speedway stars travelling the length and breadth of the country. The rider's who have benefited from his help have been the Australian Adrian Newman, Slovenian National Champion Matej Zagar and the Czech Republic aces Richard Wolf and Pavel Ondrasik. Ken has even team managed one of the Czech teams in a one off race meeting. Aged over sixty Ken keeps busy with his garage business and restoring old motorcycles. If you ask any of the speedway aces about Ken they will all say the same thing, if you wanted parts fitted, an oil change on your van, or maybe something cleaned, the job was done swiftly, and thoroughly. He is a true professional.

The older of the two brothers Dave Westaway, with Joe Sturtridge as his passenger, won the Cornish Sidecar Grass-track Junior Championship in 1970.

Dave Westaway the former speedway/grass-track competitor had to give up his career prematurely due to serious ill health problems. This is the programme cover of the benefit meeting held for him.

Two years later Dave took his first Cornish Open Sidecar Championship. Throughout the 1980s, with passenger Alan Borlase, he collected the title an incredible eight times. The duo also won the 'South-West Centre' title during this period. Fate was to deal him a heavy blow when ill health robbed him of his livelihood and his racing.

Regrettably, he is no longer with us, but he bore his illness bravely. He was a Cornish Champion, who will always be remembered and cherished. The passenger of the Westaway brothers Joe Sturtridge who today resides at Bethel, still plays an active part in helping in Cornish Grasstracks. Joe who works for one the utilities companies has given hundreds of hours of his time putting up ropes or as a flag marshal. He has helped the Par 90 club, The Mid Cornwall Premier Motorcycle Club and the Cornwall Solo Grasstrack club.

In those halcyon days of Par Moor, the outfits were in the main powered by British engines, but there were some amazing hybrids. Phil Williams used various engines including an Ariel Red Hunter, a 600cc Rudge, a J.A.P. and a 650cc Triumph twin, while the Westaway brothers used Triumph engines. Edward Kent used a 500cc Ariel Red Hunter outfit, which had an engine that

Sidecar action at Par Moor, thanks to Dave Stallworthy

on occasions could shoot out flames from the exhaust. Pat Crawford had an immaculate Vincent outfit powered by a 1000cc engine, 'which really looked the business.'

In the early years, Vic Morris of Conway Road, Falmouth stepped in to passenger Roy Wedlake or Phil Williams if they were without their regular sidecar buddies. Morris always packed his body belt and helmet just in case he was needed. In the 1960s, he rode a motorcycle with sidecar as daily transport. He will be better remembered for being the sidecar partner of Bill Uren of Glendale Crescent, Redruth. The pair were the Cornwall Centre Open Sidecar Grass-track Champions of 1963 and 1964. Morris recalled an incident one evening at the Cornish Stadium when their outfit spun around and hit the safety fence. 'It did shake us up a bit', he said.

One of Roy Wedlake's passengers in 1963 was Preston Pote from near Liskeard. Preston said, 'In my short time with Roy he was riding a J.A.P. outfit. I first competed in just one meeting with Pat Crawford, before filling in for Reg Hawken who was injured. Years later another short stint passenger was Dave Mugford. It appears Mugford had been a good friend to Roy for many years. He was only a regular for a short period. Dave is related to Alan Mugford. Dave's first cousin is better known as the musical director of the Imerys/ Eastern Area China Clay Male-Voice Choir.

Another sidecar driver was Johnny Payton, who rode a machine with an Ariel Square 4 frame and a Vincent back end, which had a Norton Dominator 88 powerhouse. Johnny became involved in speedway because of his friendship with Roland James, who was Ticker and Ken James brother.

When Payton began racing, he worked for J.H. Slade and Company, who were the well-known Cornish-based steel erectors. Phil Williams built him an outfit, which he won on at Trengwainton in 1959. John remembers practicing near the pub in Polgooth one evening, when another crew completely lost control and ended up in the pond! Johnny's passenger in sidecar speedway racing was his brother Doug. His other brother Dennis, a retired engineer who now lives in Eliot Road St.Austell recalls some of his sibling's exploits. Dennis said, "Once Doug was thrown out of the outfit at Par Moor and became entangled in the side wire fencing. Luckily he was okay." For many years Doug has lived in Australia.

It is possible another local driver participated on the evening of the 'ducking in the pond incident' he is Ken Richards of Trelowth Road, Polgooth. Together with his friend Cyril Coombe, the two only raced briefly at Par Moor, but really enjoyed it.

For Ken Richards it was very much about having a go. They raced a Matchless 500cc twin, which wasn't the ideal machine for the deep shale. Despite never winning any races, they will always remember their dabble with sidecar racing. Many years later when speedway was revived in the 1990's Ken Richards became a member of the track-staff at the Claycountry Moto Parc. Ken and his friend, the late Ron Bassett, were responsible for the excellent weather-cover, which was provided in the pit area.

Another sidecar competitor was Roger Eddy of Sladesbridge, near Wadebridge. Both he and his brother Terence rode in local trials events too. In his Cornish Stadium day's, his regular sidecar passenger was Roger Cocks. Today, he lives on the continent.

Making the journey to Par Moor from further afield were drivers Gerry Wheeler from Bridgwater and Gerry Stoneman of Tiverton. The former only had a couple of meetings riding a grass-outfit but the latter became a regular. Gerry Wheeler went on to become a British Grass-track Sidecar Champion, the

South West Champion and Wessex Champion besides winning in Germany. Gerry who first rode in 1947 still turns out occasionally riding his 1969 Lynx outfit with a Weslake engine in the Grand Slam with his son Steve. Gerry described Rhodes Minnis as his favorite track but holds Cornwall dear to his heart for the many happy times he spent in the County. Gerry was a founding father of G.R.A.S.A.(The Grass-track Riders and Supporters Association) along with other well known sidecar drivers Alan Artus and Steve Smith. Today Gerry thoroughly enjoys his hobby of vintage cars.

Gerald Stoneman however was a major influence on Gerry Wheeler's career and became part of the trapping's at Par Moor. Gerald was a mechanical genius with a tough exterior. Despite breaking several bones he continued racing against the Westaway's and Phil Williams. Gerald's nephews continue the racing legacy competing in grass-track events all over the country. Look out for Clive and Phil Stoneman in your programme! Fred Tarr also from Tiverton had several outings at Par Moor. Fred retired from racing in the late seventies and has no further contact with it.

Although Ivor Toms was better known as a 'solo rider' he did have a dabble with the sidecar speedway outfits. He raced them on and off for many years. John Luke recalls one night at Cornish Stadium when the sidecar racing was squeezed into the stock car racing programme. He continued, 'Ivor Toms throttle stuck open and they went straight into the fencing. Luckily neither Ivor or his passenger were badly hurt.' Jeremy was unable to interview Ivor's passenger Gilbert Mounce for his memories as he went abroad to live some time ago.

In April 1963, The British Sporting Sidecar Association ran it's first grass-track event in Cornwall, starting an upsurge in the sport. At the Black Cross grass-track meeting, not far from the A30, sidecar speedway drivers Phil Williams, Eddie Seymour and Ken Westaway all took part. At the end of 1963 season, solo speedway ended and the sidecar boys found their heats sandwiched between the car racing. From my research the racing just seemed to lack the same fervour and enthusiasm but despite this the riders were still paid their £5 appearance money.

Eddie Seymour who was both a sidecar driver on grass and shale became the Cornwall Secretary for the British Sporting Sidecar Association, a position he held for decades supported by his wife Gillian and daughter Esther. While Eddie was racing he thoroughly enjoyed being part of the scene but major honours were to elude him. However Eddie was well known as a motorcycle journalist, a

Ivor Toms with
son Graham
demonstrating one of
the banked outfits.

brilliant grass-track commentator, he compered many events in the Duchy and
was a presenter on B.B.C. Radio Cornwall.

When Eddie passed away in 2003 the motorcycle fraternity were stunned by
his death. He was indeed such a tireless worker for motorcycle sport. He often
marshalled, lap scored, points scored, or was an observer. He is still missed
and will never be forgotten because the author described him as 'a lovely man
and such a fountain of knowledge.' Gerry Wheeler the maestro on 3 wheels
summed up, "I had a great deal of respect for Eddie, I was glad I was able to pay
my respects to him that afternoon at Truro, the huge crowd of people doing the
same thing spoke volumes."

Looking back, probably, the most successful of all the sidecar competitors
at Par Moor was the late Phil Williams, who, in the early days used the pseud-

onym Phil Silvers. Phil's father 'Maynard' rode at Rocky Park 'with gusto' in the pioneer days.

Phil went on to be one of the most successful motorcycle competitors ever from the Duchy of Cornwall. For those of you who are too young to remember, a television comedy series ran during this period called Sergeant Bilko and its American star with a big smile was actually named Phil Silvers, he also appeared in Carry On Abroad!

Williams' wife, Rosemary, told the story of when her husband was racing a Rudge. She said: 'On six days of the week Phil just couldn't start the machine, but come Tuesday evening it always fired up. I could never understand it!' John Lawer of Biscovey, who is a second cousin to Williams, rode briefly with him at Par Moor. John openly talked to the author about his cousin. He said:'Phil and I grew up together, we practiced 'the cycle speedway sliding technique' on the stadium car park at Par Moor. We spent many a happy hour on our pushbikes! When we were a little older, we had an A.J.S. 500 cc motorcycle, which was used as a field bike.' Today Frank Hawke still owns this 1927 bike.

He continued: 'I recall it had to have its clutch done. We went to a chemist and bought some corks, and with some help from Roy Wedlake, got the clutch working smoothly. I was working on the farm by the time I rode with Phil.

When David Stephens had measles, I stepped in to fill the gap. I also recall doing some scrambles meetings with him too. During the spell I was riding with Phil I had become a Dad and my family were not keen I was a passenger to him, because he was just like his father, Maynard, totally fearless!'

Brian Jose of Hayle, a former employee of Ash and Lacey, was another stand in passenger for Phil Williams. Brian was a grass-track passenger for both Geoffrey Riggs and Bill Uren. When Brian rode with Phil he was never known by his real name, the programme usually read 'Phil Silvers' and 'Yogi Bear'. Brian recalls two sides to his former speedway/grass-track colleague. He said, "When I had a bad racing accident at the Mountain Grass-track at Portreath I was flat on my back for three months, my future looked bleak. Phil Williams came to see me in Truro hospital to cheer me up. In contrast on the track 'Phil' was hard and highly competitive, if he saw a gap he went through it."

A later speedway passenger, Alan Martin of St.Austell, who was Phil William's hillclimb and road-racing partner concurred with Brian's views. He said, Phil rode with a determination and would ride around or over anyone. With the backing of major sponsorship Phil could have been bidding for the World

Phil Williams pictured here trialing in 1957 at Colwith Farm, the property of the Dustow family. Phil within a couple of years would be racing on the shale every Tuesday night, photo David Stephens.

Phil Williams was not just a speedway sidecar competitor. At the weekends he also excelled in scrambling, trials and grass-track. Here is Phil with David Stephens at the Madron Scramble in 1960. Note the Berkeley in the background, reg.no.744 HCV. The three-wheeler had a 328cc Excelsior Talisman twin engine. Incidently both lads were 22 years old when photographed.

Sidecar Road Race title, he had the ability and courage to do it."

Phil Williams motorcycle career started when he became a solo trials champion, then a successful sidecar trials rider, followed by being a Cornish Grass-track Sidecar Champion, and a National Hillclimb Champion and runner-up in the British Sidecar Road Racing Championship in the short span of a year. He went on to compete in international road racing throughout the United Kingdom against the world's greatest exponents. With long-time passenger and good friend Alan Martin, he completed two successful campaigns at the Isle of Man TT. Regrettably, his third attempt ended in tragedy, when Williams was badly hurt in a racing accident, while his passenger, Steve Verne from Havant, died of his injuries.

The author and his wife Shirley were in the Island at the time supporting their friend. They visited him in Nobles hospital Douglas and again when he returned to Cornwall. After a break of about a year, Phil Williams returned to racing action. The diminutive and highly spirited rider came back to ride in hillclimbs, sprints and in solo-road racing, representing Cornwall in the Celtic Five Nations Series.

Unfortunately, in 2005 Phil passed away after losing his battle with cancer. Phil was just sixty-eight years of age and despite being so poorly at the end, never lost his great sense of humour or his love of being kept up to date with his interests in motorcycling and steam engines. On his sixty-eighth birthday, he received a card which made him chuckle. It stated Ariels were rode by real men! Some of us are old enough to remember the marque! Incidentally, even today his family still own the Ariel outfit which Phil raced all those years ago, securely locked away I might add!

His passing was a sad loss for author Jeremy Jackson personally, because he had known and supported Phil Williams since the age of seventeen, travelling to many race meetings with him and Alan Martin. Indeed, if he hadn't met the multi-talented racer, Jackson doubts if he would have ever written any 'motor-sport books' or run any charity bike shows. Jerry said, "I can still picture the tiny figure of Phil coming into work on an 850cc Moto-Guzzi. He did many a job for home in his lunch breaks.

In my opinion Phil becoming a diabetic in later life never hampered his track career. He just got on with routine things. He was a true Cornishman loving simple things like a pint of ale, a game of euchre and walking across the field on a summer morning!"

Phil Williams and Alan Martin were competitors in sidecar speedway at Par Moor. Later they became National Hillclimb sidcar champions. Then they accepted the ultimate challenge of competing in international sidecar road racing, photo Jeremy Jackson.

One of Phil's passengers, Edward Kent had his own speedway outfit too. Walter Dawson, a retired engineer who lives at Fowey described Edward as 'completely mad on a bike in his younger day.' Edward rode in trials, besides doing some speedway racing. Edward even managed to edge Clive Dustow of Par out of his own workshop in those trials days, poor Clive was relegated to the milking parlour. In one Bude to Lands End Trial, Edward borrowed his brother-in-laws bike a B.S.A. Goldflash. Unfortunately Walter broke down on the B.S.A. C15 so he jumped aboard with Edward and the two finished the trial 'two up'.

Many tales of Phil William's passengers survive despite him not being around to share in the mirth.

One of Phil's friends and passengers in hillclimbing was John Hill who worked for 'Marshalls'. John also helped Edward Kent behind the scenes. John was a talented engineer who had oxygen and acetylene bottles in his workshop so his modifications were sought after. Some years later John became the Fowey Ports

Engineer for English China Clays where he had the reputation as a 'speedster'. He was the only guy to totally trash an 'Austin Maxi' in the Pinnock Tunnel, which joined the ports of Par and Fowey. Originally it had been a rail link but was later turned into a haul road.

The Pinnock Tunnel came up in my conversation with Phil William's former passenger David Stephens. David was coaxed into being the passenger when Phil was testing out his road race outfit on the E.C.L.P. private road. Having sought the permissions Phil drove the outfit through the tunnel like a bat out of hell. Brian Martin was chasing them in his own car but failed to keep up. David said he felt like 'jelly' when he got off. Although on reflection he had no fear in Phil's ability and would have ridden to the ends of the earth with him. David recalled how he started riding with Phil Williams all those years ago. He said, 'Our partnership started in 1960, I was earning just £11 a week as a plumber.' 'One of the first outfit's we assembled was a Ariel Red Hunter which cost us £11-10-0 (£11-50) The bike came from a guy in the village of Bugle costing £9 and the sidecar unit came from John Hill who charged us £2-10-0 (£2-50) We rode a variety of machines in grass-track, scrambles, and speedway. Racing in speedway in the early days Phil rode a Rudge, I think it had the Ulster Special engine. Well to get over the problem with the exhaust lift one exhaust port was plugged up. With the heat and Phil's driving, the plug blew out and went flying off into the crowd. We certainly had our share of thrills and spills.'

David continued, 'The worst scrapes I had personally with him were grass-track racing and scrambling' Once I was badly concussed at Sinns Barton and I was extremely lucky at Madron when I fell out of the chair when Phil was doing a speed of 60-70 m.p.h. I lay on the ground and Roger Eddy brilliantly took preventative action to miss me.'

Fred Paul of Sheviock recalled going to watch a stock car meeting in this period accompanied by his friend Bernard Harding. He particularly remembered watching Pat Crawford and Ken Westaway race. He said: 'Pat Crawford was a character, although I didn't see it myself he allegedly put a B.S.A. A7 engine in a lawnmower, I reckon he brought formula one to motor mowers!' Sadly Pat Crawford's sidecar passenger, Vic Skinner was not available for interview because he passed away in 1995.

In 1965, drivers Phil Williams, Ivor Toms, Pat Crawford and Roy Wedlake raced at Exeter's County Ground circuit, going head-to-head with Australian visitors Harry Denton and Brian O'Shea. The first race went the way of Den-

Pat Crawford leads at Par Moor.

ton, while O'Shea took victory in the next. In the third heat, Denton crashed with Phil Williams and his outfit went over the top of the safety fencing, but luckily no one was seriously injured.

Tragically, four years later, Denton died in a racing accident in his native Australia. A great loss to motor-sport.

In the sixties Alan Jenkins who today resides at Old Roselyon Road, Par recalls his first visit to watch the car racing and the sidecars. "I was very taken by the noise and spectacle of it all." Years later his son Simon helped mechanic for Paul and Mark Westaway from Par who were cousins to the sidecar competitors of Carclaze.

Roy Wedlake was truly a shale shifter and loved riding at the County Ground or Wembley. Sadly his results were never as good when the Par Moor surface became tarmac. During my research I unearthed some letters sent to Roy Wedlake by Gerry Dommett Promotions of Fordingbridge confirming bookings for the sidecar speedway outfits for Bristol, on Good Friday(31st March) and Bank Holiday Monday (28th.August 1972).

One of the other local riders that also drove in sidecars and combined it with solo riding was Eric Roberts, who now resides in the holiday and surf resort of Newquay. Eric Roberts was a great friend of both Chris Julian and Eric Martyn.

Both were also very actively involved at Par Moor. Eric Roberts rode mainly in local events because of his work commitments. Having established an asphalt and tarmacadam laying business in 1950, Eric found it awkward to commit fully to racing due to obvious personal and financial constraints. He also had an interest in stock car racing and had some involvement in this in later years. Eric Robert's sidecar passenger, Michael Johns recalled his racing days. He said, "Nearly all the riding gear I had was borrowed from different people. The leather boots I wore were miles too big for me, as were the over trousers. This was the sixties, I was young but we so enjoyed being part of it." Today, Michael still has an interest in grass-track and speedway and will be often spotted in the crowd.

A solo rider who excelled in sidecar racing as a passenger was Reg Hawken, who won many accolades with the late Roy Wedlake. The Porthpean-born racer rode for St.Austell Gulls on an ex Lloyd Goffe J.A.P. He also turned out a couple times for Plymouth. With the demise of speedway, he followed his hankering for other things and took up driving stock cars, successfully qualifying for the World Finals in 1969, 1971 and 1973. If you thought charging around in a stock car is dangerous, think again, there are people like Reg Hawken who will try anything!

Reg then went into auto stunts for three years, doing things like car jumping and rollovers, while his party piece involved smashing through a furniture van at high speed. Not content with these endeavours, he also drove karts with some success, mainly at Dunkeswell on a KTM 250cc kart. Over the years, he has always loved speedway though and said Barry Briggs was his all-time favourite, although when he was a schoolboy, Reg thought the Australians Allan Quinn and Jack Gates were great. 'They were my idols', he said. He was a regular spectator at Exeter speedway. In 1997 he first supported the new St.Austell B.W.O.C. Gulls followed by the Trelawny JAG Tigers at Claycountry, Nanpean. Reg has now made an excellent recovery from surgery on his knee. He said, "I broke plenty of bones riding speedway but this knee has certainly put me through the pain barrier. I will now be able to enjoy walking our dog again!"

Someone else who dabbled in sidecar speedway at Par Moor was Alan Rowe of Lostwithiel. He was a self-employed lorry driver who participated in the early years. Alan Rowe's passenger was Dave Stone. When Stone wasn't available to

The late Roy Wedlake, people will always remember him.

partner him, Dave Abbiss stepped into the breach to ride in the chair. The lads used a 500cc Vincent with a hand built frame. It appeared to have plenty of power for the straight, but was difficult to handle when cornering. The interest didn't run in the family though, as his brother Ashley, who now resides in Bodmin didn't share his sibling's passion for bikes. Regrettably, Alan Rowe passed away in 2003 after a battle with serious illness.

Another name linked with Par Moor is former Sidecar Grass-track Junior Champion Tyrone Snell but not on three wheels! Tyrone Snell from Longdowns drove in Hot Rod classes across the South West of England.

The Par Moor track closed for stock car and banger racing in 1986 and the last of the sidecars disappeared as well. People had their memories, some kept race programmes and a few had taken photographs of their sporting heroes. The speedway stadium was flattened to make way for a shopping complex.

In 1994, the sidecars made a brief return at the White Gold Classic and Custom Bike Show, which ran in Westhaul Park. The Heavy Transport yard virtually opposite the old speedway stadium had seen lots of changes in forty years. The sound of the three outfits circulating in the small demonstration ring certainly brought back memories and a definite whiff up the nose! Of course the transport yard in the boom years at one time had been home to nearly 400 lorries, serving the china clay fleet throughout the United Kingdom.

After the return of speedway to Cornwall at Claycountry Moto Parc, the outfits made a brief reappearance under the organization of enthusiast and competitor Ken Westaway. Three outfits were again demonstrated on 25 August 1998.

The 1994 White Gold Classic and Custom Bike Show organized by the author brought memories flooding back. Here are the three surviving outfits from the sixties, photo Ted Davies.

The competitors were the Westaway family, together with Australian speedway star Adrian Newman, Phil Williams and hillclimb passenger Tony Stephens, and finally by Ken's sons Justin and Wayne. Surprisingly, Newman had never ridden an outfit in his life, but he did remarkably well considering his inexperience. The heats were shared, Williams took the first and Ken Westaway the second, while the Westaway brothers took the flag in the third and fourth heats.

It is worthy of noting a passenger of Wayne Westaway at the Claycountry Moto-Parc in only just one meeting was Patrick Nolan. Pat had this to say about his experience with the old Aussie banked sidecar outfits, "I found it a bit weird, it was indeed an eye opener which gave me a huge respect for the people who used to race at Cornish Stadium."

Ken Westaway said he wished to dedicate the evening's racing to his step-son Phil Pitman, who lost his life on 6 May 1996 in a sidecar racing accident at Abingdon in Oxfordshire. Phil Pitman, when partnered by Redruth's Myles Simmons, had become the Cornish Centre Sidecar Grass-track Champion's in 1995. They were also runners-up in the British Best Pairs, as well as being fifth in the British Masters in 1995. Indeed, Pitman was a remarkable young man

Ken Westaway(left) and sidecar passenger Adrian Newman.

with such a zest for life. He had a bright future in the sport and was making sufficient progress to become the new British Sidecar Champion, but it wasn't to be. At work, Phil Pitman laboured hard in his building business with his cousin Rob Craddock. Phil excelled when racing karts with his friends, and on a squash court he was a formidable opponent.

In the world of motorcycle-sport, he was one of the elite, a real professional in the preparation of his machine and a true sportsman. He was always positive and determined to succeed. Despite what life threw at him he always sported a smile! Following his tragic passing, his mum, Mrs.Carol Pitman, helped by family and friends, formed the Par 90 Grass-track Club, which kept her son's memory alive.

They organised two successful meetings for charity. The first event, at Retallick Park near St Columb Major in March 1997, was a great success. However, the second at South Tregleath Farm, Washaway in September 1999 was an even greater success. The proceeds for charity swelled to over £10,000. This was a truly remarkable achievement by everyone concerned, a fitting tribute to a very special young man. Phil Pitman touched so many people's lives' so he will never be forgotten by the folk of mid Cornwall!

Ken and son's Justin and Wayne Westaway plus Aussie ace Adrian Newman sporting the B.W.O.C. Gulls race jacket, photos John Yeo, Terras.

Despite Cornish Stadium at Par Moor being just a memory, many sidecar racers who live and work in Cornwall have tried their hand in the sport in recent years. The author expands a little further on their successes. Ken Curnow and Steve Harman, the 1996 British Pre 75 Grass-track Sidecar Champions had a flirtation with the shale, before going back to road racing. In 2000 they won four races at the Claycountry Moto Parc and took one heat at the B.M.F. Rally at Peterborough. Wayne Westaway and Mark Courtney have tried the sport, but continued to concentrate on their love of grass-track racing. The crew have since parted company, with Wayne trying out a new racing passenger.

Helston's Richard Thomas, along with passenger Kevin Woodley competed in the British Championship in 2002 and 2003. They did experience some moderate success winning a B final in 2002.

Also in 2002 Richard and Kevin won a guest meeting at the Oak Tree Arena, Highbridge in Somerset. Richard said, "My first love is grass-track racing so we concentrated on what we knew well". Today, Richard continues sidecar racing.

He has used two other passengers, namely Jason Barry and Terry Saunters. It would take another crew to take the sport to greater heights and we give you an update on their progress in a following chapter.

Drivers and their hometown in the sixties

Passengers

Roy Wedlake (St. Austell)

Reg Hawken, Vic Skinner,
Vic Morris, Preston Pote,
and Dave Mugford.

Pat Crawford (Saltash)

Vic Skinner and Pete Stacey

Alan Humphries (Padstow)

Jim Crews

Phil Williams alias Phil Silvers (Tywardreath)

David Stephens, Vic Morris,
John Lawer, Alan Sheen alias
Cheyenne, Edward Kent,
Brian Jose alias Yogi Bear,
and Alan Martin.

Eric Roberts (Fraddon)

Michael Johns

Gerald Stoneman (Tiverton)

Pat Jones and Stuart Rattenbury

Fred Tarr (Tiverton)

Stuart Rattenbury and
Brian Buckingham

Ivor Toms (Stenalees)

Gilbert Mounce and Alan Libby

Ken Westaway alias Ken West (St. Austell)

Alan Libby and Joe Sturtridge

David Westaway alias Dave West (St. Austell)

Joe Sturtridge

Eddie Seymour (Helston)

John Trevaskis

Johnny Payton (St. Austell)

Doug Payton and Terry Beard

Roger Eddy (Sladesbridge, near Wadebridge)

Roger 'Ginger' Cocks

Edward Kent (Par)

Billy Holder

Alan Rowe (Lostwithiel)

Dave Stone and Dave Abbiss

Ken Richards (Polgooth)

Cyril Coombe

Gerry Wheeler (Bridgwater)

Reg Granville

Taken before its demolition in the late eighties. The facilities had been in decline for many years, photos John Jarvis, Bristol.

Tales of Roger, Charlie, Dowie, Barry and Martin

The author has already assembled a vast collection of anecdotes, now motorcycle enthusiast Roger Fogg from Lanjeth adds his memories. Roger explained it was more than forty years ago, but the memories are still fresh although perhaps some of the details are a little hazy. "We would all meet at the village of London Apprentice, around 7 o'clock on a Tuesday evening, and go up "the Moors" on the old winding road towards St.Austell. Just after the Iron Bridge we would turn right up through Trevarrick, and in turn go through Charlestown, finally emerging at Cypress Avenue opposite Par Stadium. Tuesday night was of course Stock Car Racing. We were Charlie, Dowie, Barry, Martin and myself. We rode half-decent big British Bikes, some slightly better kept than others, but all cherished! Barry and Dowie bought their B.S.A. Super Rockets in the same year. Barry's sported a large red Avonaire fairing that was usually liberally coated with farm detritus from Tregenna Lane and the farms down there. On the other hand Dowie, who whistled constantly as he rode, had a Jaguar emblem on his front mudguard, a pair of Gold Star silencers and a full set of gleaming chrome crash bars. Martin had a B.S.A. A7, then later a Norton Dominator; Charlie had a new Triumph Tiger 90, and I had Triumph Speedtwin in aramanth red and cream Dulux.

Cypress Avenue was a concrete road, and the tall trees that lined the road on each side provided excellent leaning posts for the bikes, also these were of course free as opposed to having to pay to park in the Stadium itself. Already there could be heard the clatter of unsilenced engines being revved up in the pits. The chain link and galvanise fence that surrounded the high sandy banks dividing the track from the car parking area had a small entrance guarded by a tin shed and a form of turnstile. There were some 'nere do wells' that got in through gaps in the fences, but we never did, always paying honestly for our evenings entertainment. Pushing through 'the entrance' we would enter the arena itself. There, spread out before us, was the track, with a green coloured grand stand on one side, and at the far end, next to the Britannia Inn, the pit area. The old loudspeaker van played scratchy, ever so slightly old fashioned hits of the day between announcements and commentaries. "I'm in pieces, bits and pieces" it would crackle out. The smell of the fried onions from the hot dog stall, (there were only ever hot dogs on sale; burgers not having been invented at the time) mingled with the petrol fumes, and there seemed to be onion and tomato ketchup splattered coats and mouths everywhere. Friends and acquaintances would be greeted, regulars who each week turned out to watch their favourite drivers and cars do battle with each other. There was then, as there is now, an army of knowledgeable enthusiasts who were not afraid to voice their opinions on any subject.

At around 7.25 p.m., the noise from the pits began to grow in volume, and in equal degrees smoke and steam were observed billowing across the crowd, or towards the 'Pub', depending on wind direction. On the stroke of 7.30 p.m., and probably not a minute too soon, the crescendo of sound reached deafening point and onto the track to begin the first of the many races would come the cars. They were spectacular of course, sliding, skidding, a blur of garish colours and flapping roof numbers, flying shale, mostly going forwards, sometimes sideways or backwards and not infrequently vertically upward.

There was a cheer as one went completely upside down. This continued for an hour or so, I never completely understood the scoring system, neither did I care much, but all concerned seemed to be having a good time as long as the cars stayed their side of the rather flimsy looking wire safety ropes. However all this was a mere prelude to the real fun of the evening, the sidecar races! Real speedway had disappeared some years before, and all that remained was this peculiar style of motor cycle racing that in many ways was quite unique.

Advance warning of the appearance of the sidecars was given by a different kind of noise in the pits. A Triumph on open pipes would start up, tentatively at first on one cylinder then building to a full throated roar as the second cylinder chimed in. This was followed by similar noises from the other competing outfits all having their throttles blipped, getting the motors nice and warm. The glorious smell of Castrol "R" would begin to waft across the crowds, the start of the sidecar racing was announced and onto the track would come the four pairs of competitors. The sidecars at the time were strange hybrids, designed to be run in one direction, clockwise only. Standing still they looked as if they were cornering hard. The frames, perhaps ex.war-department Ariels or rigid Triumphs were welded securely to the very basic sidecar chassis. The frame tilted inward, and the banked sidecar wheel was attached at an even more acute angle. There was a tiny petrol tank, which was almost an afterthought, an oil reservoir of a kind, and a monstrous great engine to drive the thing. Gearbox and clutch were basic, chains barely covered, with minimalist seating and mudguards. The small platform that the passenger clung to had wooden slats and hand holds welded onto the bikes frame. Paint and general finish were never a strong point, these were hard working machines, mechanically excellent but blues, yellows and reds were applied as a kind of optional extra, a long way from todays hi tech finishes with sponsorship logos and corporate advertising. The girder forks had side struts to prevent them from flexing, or home made Earles-type devices, which did the same job. They were mean, purposeful, no nonsense motorcycles designed with but a single purpose, which was to get in front and stay there for enough laps to beat all the others.

The men who rode the bikes were sometimes flamboyant characters, sometimes quiet and inscrutable, but they all shared the drive and will to be first past the chequered flag. Roy Wedlake was not known as 'Shaker' for nothing, he had been shaken and stirred more than anyone, even fracturing his skull in his racing career, yet he still came back for more. Phil Williams was quiet and thoughtful, but full of steely determination. He may have inherited some of this from his father Maynard, a local undertaker, who used to treat unsuspecting passengers in his own vintage sidecar by taking them to Par Docks and aviating the third wheel whilst hanging it out over the edge of the dock wall.

The Westaway brothers were skilled engineers who raced a variety of outfits very successfully. All were black suited heroes as far as we were concerned. Then there were the passengers, who were indeed a race apart. They had to know their drivers, put utter faith in their judgements and abilities, and be prepared to perform the most agile of movements in double quick time in order to prevent the whole outfit tipping up or crashing.

The flag would drop and as the engines roared the drivers would scrabble to keep the front wheel on the ground and the power on song. With bars twitching and shale flying the four outfits seemed as one as they entered the first corner. Wheels touched, passengers hung on for dear life, smoke billowed, and grit scattered. Gradually one would draw away from the others, perhaps by only a little, but enough for the chorus of noise to become uneven as each outfit sang its own song. The colours of the bikes and their riders would gradually turn

Phil Williams and passenger Alan Martin at Par Moor 1969.

to one as, particularly if it were a wet evening, everything would be covered in what was basically mud."

Sometimes they might get tangled, none would give way after all, and on occasion there might be a mechanical breakdown or even a more serious incident. Honours at the end always seemed to be even, and there would eventually be a winner declared although this could not necessarily be predicted on a regular basis. All too soon the sidecar races would be over and it would be back to the stock cars again. At this point we would generally watch a few more of the cars going around, but we had seen what we wanted to see, and we often left before the end to avoid the traffic. With night falling and with the parlous state of our electrics we had had a good evening's entertainment, and would probably be back the following week for more."

Today, Roger who lives at Lanjeth is known locally as a prolific writer of motoring and historical books. He is the current chairman of the Cornwall Section of the Vintage Motorcycle Club. He said that he now prefers to work less hours, so he can enjoy family life with wife Mignon, daughters Leah and Tatum and his grandchildren.

2006 Sidecar update

In the year 2001, a new sidecar partnership was born in Cornish grass-track. Matthew Tyrrell and Shaun Yates were on a journey that would take them to Centre honours, National honours and fulfilling a dream of racing in Australia. Shaun had some experience in the sidecar racing having been a passenger with Roche's Andy Symons. Shaun felt it was time to move on for personal reasons and he has never looked back.

Both men had sporting Dad's to be proud of. Shaun's Dad, Peter Yates rode as a passenger to Alan Sheen in Cornish Grasstrack's. Sadly Alan died whilst the author was putting the finishing touches to this book. In 1968 they were the Cornish Sidecar Junior Champions. Likewise Matt's Dad, Chris was a successful sidecar competitor. Chris was a Cornish Open Sidecar Champion in the nineties partnered by Alan Borlase. Chris is still very actively involved in the sport. He is Cornwall Centre A.C.U. Chairman and was a founder member of the hugely successful Mid Cornwall Premier Motorcycle Club who host the annual Westcountry Winner. They hosted the prestigious British Masters Grasstrack at Rumford, near Padstow in September 2006.

Following successes in grass-track racing, Matt and Shaun also took up Sidecar Speedway. They started with a Steer frame but found it wasn't for them. They had remarkable improvement when moving to a Russell Mitchell copy. Their reputation in grass-track was on the up and up. Success came via being Cornish Open Champions, the Junior winners at 'The Jim Coles Spectacular', winners of the 'Salisbury Sizzler' and taking a win at Memmingham in Germany.

In sidecar speedway the pair were battling it out with John Halsey, Ivor Matthews, Rob Wilson, John Hiscock, and a few lesser known names who fancied their chances. In 2005, Matt and Shaun brought the British Speedway title back to Cornwall for the first time. They shared the title with Ivor Matthews and Mick Stace. They both competed in eight rounds and finished with ninety-eight points. It was the first time ever the trophy had been shared.

Matthew said they were the fastest crew around the Exeter County Ground. The County Ground banked circuit, which has since closed down was the fastest track in England. Matt and Shaun commented they both liked racing at Exeter as it was close to home for them and also they rode well there. No-one knows what will happen in racing though, and when they were going well in the Isle of Wight whilst heading for the line they had a puncture dropping them to fourth place.

The 2005 racing season was made of magic for the two Cornish building contractors. With sponsorship of a bike from Ian and Jan Mills of Reading (MCP Racing) they have been highly competitive. With other good sponsors on board like Paul Miller Racing, Lynd and Co Racing, PDQ and Ken Hicks Tuning the Yamaha FZR has performed well. Besides winning the British title they were joint leaders of the British Qualifier, they took first in the Longtrack in Vilsoven and second in the British averages throughout the season. Incidently, Matt is a partner with his Dad, Chris in the family building business. Shaun works independently as a builder/plasterer throughout the U.K.

What was next for the British Championship title-holders? They weren't going to sit back, they decided to go for it, to live the dream, to try to conquer the Australian tracks. Matt describes his experience 'Down Under' as 'fantastic'.

Matthew and Shaun set out to ride a few of the Australian events. Shaun set his sights on touring Australia in a camper van where he thoroughly enjoyed himself. Something he will always recall doing.

Matt and family were made welcome by his host Andrew Cleave at Shepparton. Matt and Shaun are the first British crew to tour Australia and without a shadow of doubt the most successful of all time. They took in four meetings in just under a month. Matt's photograph even appeared on the front cover of the Shepparton Car Weekly newspaper. Back home Matt and Shaun were deservedly featured on the cover of the 2006 Cornwall Centre Handbook

On the 7 January at the Victoria State Championship, at Undera they were winners but fate dealt them a heavy blow when they were unfairly excluded. Matt said, 'We were excluded on a minor technicality because we couldn't see the pole line, frankly there wasn't one'. In the second half racing again they went well, coming runners up in the Memorial Meeting.

A week later on the 14 January the lads from Cornwall competed in the Victoria Sidecar Shoot out at Mildura. They did well taking third place overall.

With just a few days break on the 21 January they were riding at the State Motorcycle Complex at Broadford. In searing heat of over 40 degrees celsius Matthew and Shaun took three wins, and one third. They had beaten one of the best Aussie drivers, Warren Monson, and won the meeting on countback.

The icing on the cake was being invited to compete in the 'Australian

Matt Tyrrell and Shaun Yates who put Cornwall on the map for grass-track and speedway.

Sidecar Speedway Championship' on 27 January at Gosford City. At this highly important meeting, they were pitched against top drivers like, Victoria title-holder Bevan Gates, Mick Headland, Warren Monson, Jayden Mayes, Jason Bradshaw, Malcolm German and Dion Lynd. Not fazed by the heat or the stiff competition they were placed 'twelfth' overall against the world's best sidecar competitors.

In 2006, Matt and Shaun continued competing in events at home and abroad. They were in action locally at the Westcountry Winner on 7 May at Pentruse Farm near Wadebridge. All went well in the speedway sidecar heats (on grass), in the second leg they went from third to first in one swift manoeuvre. In 'the sidecar speedway final' they were 'pipped' to the chequered flag by Ivor Matthews and Ben Goddard. Unfortunately, they did not take a rostrum place in the sidecar grass-track, which was scooped by the 2005 winners, Myles Simmons and Kevin Woodley.

It would prove a busy year working hard in the building trade during the week and riding most weekends. Their big meetings included many UK venues, the long trip to Poland and competing in 'The British Masters' in September.

Sadly, a Masters rostrum place eluded the pair who today live only a few miles apart, the driver at Hallew near Bugle and passenger at Lanjeth respectively. In the heats they had two thirds, a fourth, and once unplaced. Unfortunately, they didn't assemble enough points to make the cut for the final, which was won by Rob Bradley and Shaun Simpson from Slingsby.

Rob Wilson of Headcorn who had won the championship twice before and passenger Nicky Owen were runners-up. In the 'British Sidecar-speedway Championship' Matthew and Shaun fought for points tooth and nail. With just two rounds left to run, Gary Jackson and Carl Blyth led the championship on eleven points. Matt was equal second on ten points with drivers Myles Simmons of Redruth and Ivor Matthews from Ashorne.

The final round was at Swindon Speedway, which Matthew and Shaun won but it wasn't quite enough to beat Jackson and Blyth who took the title for 2006. Matthew and Shaun were very worthy runners-up.

The sidecar aces continue to race on a regular basis. Their last home event in 2006 was 'The Bonfire Burn-up', yet another big U.K. grass-track extravaganza. Matt and Shaun finished in third place behind Rob Wilson/Nicky Owen who just had 'the edge' on the day.

In 2007 Matthew and Shaun started their sidecar campaign riding in the 'Westcountry Winner.' The Mid Cornwall Premier event moved to a new venue at Bocadden Farm, near Pelynt with a rather different but challenging track. In their first heat of the afternoon they were relegated to third place. The next heat saw a real scrap for second place with Matt Fumarola and Andi Wilson. Tyrrell cleverly shut the door on his opponent as he tried every way to get by on the last lap. Another heat win and second place secured the Cornish based crew an 'A Final' place. The 'A Final' winners were Duncan Tolhurst and Terry Saunters, but Matt and Shaun were worthy runners up. Myles Simmons and Kevin Woodley also made the rostrum. Hopefully this is a good omen for Matt and Shaun who have built a reputation of being more than just a local sidecar crew. How do you sum up an article when a racing career is still developing?

All you can say is well done lads, the Mid Cornwall Premier Motorcycle club are proud of you as are everyone you have touched in your short and successful track career. Tyrrell and Yates have certainly put Cornwall on the map regarding sidecar racing. Jackson said, 'If you don't believe me ask the spectator at Broadford, he's seen the 'flying Poms' in action!'

Was Clever Trevor, the last of the showmen?

Trevor Redmond passed away in 1997 just after his seventieth birthday. Motorsport had lost another great and colourful character. Trevor played a key and pivotal role in promoting speedway and stock car racing. He had many hidden talents, including the ability to adapt to many different situations'. He could watch his P's and Q's with distinguished guests or he could swear like a kid from the backstreet with the drivers in the pits. He was not a timid man and would not hold back when two drivers were brawling, he would wade in and separate them. Trevor was a man of wit with a dry sense of humour.

In the next few page's we hope to bring you an insight into the man who from starting as a successful rider became a manager, promoter, mentor, and a member of the F.I.M. for New Zealand, his native country. T.R. was born in Christchurch on 16 June 1927. Before he came to England, his job description was that of a 'wool classer'. Former England star Eric Boocock likened him to Keith Waterhouse's character Billy Liar but the author is of the opinion 'T.R. had much more of Johnnie Hoskins in him as 'Johnnie, the Showman' was his idol'. Trevor was always the life and soul of the party, shrieks of laughter would constantly be heard from the table where T.R. sat.

Trevor Redmond's first motorcycle as a teenager was a belt drive Douglas. When he was seventeen years of age, he replaced it with a 250c.c.model. T.R. soon dabbled in trials riding and had a go on a dirt-trotting track. He was hooked and became involved in a big way. T.R. was so enthusiastic to keep the local track alive he founded the Tai Tapu Motor Club. This was the kick which New Zealand motorsport needed. Trevor was also responsible for bringing Midget cars from North Island.

In 1950 he came to England where he soon 'honed up' his riding skill's with the help of Mike Erskine, Jon Erskine's father. After becoming an overnight success with Aldershot 'Shots' T.R. the Division III Match Race Champion moved to Wembley Lions for a record fee. T.R. had beaten Ken Middleditch twice, Don Hardy, Terry Small and Alan Smith each once to claim the Championship. In his first season at Wembley Trevor scored an incredible 233 League points. Trevor's Kiwi pal Geoff Mardon went to ride at Wimbledon and the Aldershot side collapsed. At the end of the 1952 season, 'The Shots' withdrew from the League, no Trevor, hence no League club!

T.R. first met Pat Netcott at Aldershot, they later married at St.Austell Registry office. During this time he helped and mentored his 'up and coming countryman' Barry Briggs who was to set the world of speedway on fire. After his first successful year at Aldershot, Trevor returned home to New Zealand. He was 'tickled pink' to show Barry Briggs his new Austin A70 car and Matchless twin motorcycle. Barry was impressed and agreed to come to England. Briggs had ridden in cycle speedway with Ronnie Moore and been around bikes for many years. Barry's parents had split up and his mother didn't like bike racing so she had to be persuaded to let her son go. When 'Briggo' arrived in England he stayed with T.R. at Sutton and joined Wimbledon Dons. Briggs was still legally 'a minor' so Trevor was named as his guardian. The seventeen-year old bloomed at the Plough Lane track and also Shelbourne Park.

In 1954, T.R. had progressed to riding in the World Final at Wembley. He only scored five points but was indeed riding in prestigious company. T.R.s best position in the World Individual Championship was fourth place. Sadly, a rostrum place was to elude him. Trevor showed early on he had 'bags of confidence, he could multi-task and became a resilient man. Following Bruce Abernethy's lead Trevor Redmond introduced his form of 'the Haka' when the Kiwi's rode. He loved entertaining and when he took the New Zealand side to South Africa he was in his element and even did 'the Haka' in his underpants.

The Kiwis had so much talent during this fifties period in the shape of, Ronnie Moore, Bruce Abernethy, Geoff Mardon, Ron Johnston, Bob Duckworth, Laurie Holland, Mick Holland, Bryce Subritzsky, Barry Briggs and of course T.R. Trevor loved the banter between the lads and took great delight in Geoff Mardon's suggestion they could hammer a team from China. T.R. was always game to dress up so wearing the hooped black and white rugby shirt for test matches came easy to him, so did wearing the matador's outfit on the South Africa tour.

T.R. enjoyed telling the story of how he travelled back after one meeting with Ray Cresp. They were travelling at speed on roads they didn't know with Ray at the wheel, when they went around a corner too fast and hit a railway bridge at seventy miles per hour. The Morris 1000 stood on its end and the bikes fell on Ray and Trevor. Ray was badly concussed. T.R. thought, "I can't die here because I've got £1000 in cash in my pocket." At about 3 a.m. T.R. 'flagged down' a car, the occupants summoned an ambulance, and both riders woke up in hospital no worse for their experience.

In 1955, Cornish Stadium was standing empty. T.R. drove down to Cornwall in a new Chevrolet to view the venue. He could see some potential at Par Moor. In August 1955, T.R. promoted Stock car racing at Cornish Stadium for the first time with his future father-in-law, Bob Netcott. T.R. often used 'a term of endearment' to Robert even on the microphone and often referred to him as 'Uncle Bob'. Trevor breathed life back into Cornish speedway by reviving the St.Austell Gulls in 1958. The Open Meetings blended well with car racing. Meanwhile Trevor was still enjoying riding in speedway. Trevor didn't spend a great deal of time on bike preparation but had the ability to still go out and win races.

Never one to miss an opportunity T.R. spotted someone filming with a cine-camera at Par Moor. It might have been the sixties but he wasn't slow to claim a Hollywood producer was preparing a speedway film at his track.

With the disappointment of the failure of his Neath project in 1962 T.R. bounced back to keep the Provincial speedway team together riding at Par Moor. A year later he took the St.Austell Gulls into the Provincial League. With poor weather and falling crowd's Trevor decided to take his promotion for speedway to Glasgow. He continued riding speedway and kept a foothold in Cornwall by keeping stock car racing and sidecars going. Who but someone like Trevor Redmond could persuade Chris Julian and Ray Wickett to ride for him at White City? What a round trip!

Tales are told 'on both sides of the border' of Cornishman Chris Julian being so exhausted with the travelling he was found asleep in a cardboard box.

Peter Rundle, a speedway fan of the sixties period commented, "Without Trevor Redmond we would not have had any speedway at Par Moor, he made it happen!" Peter loved his speedway and used to attend meetings with Mike Hocking. Today Peter is unable to attend race meetings due to ill health but still has a keen interest through reading books and watching televised events.

In 1965 Trevor finally hung up his leathers and concentrated on promoting full-time. He had ridden for clubs all around the United Kingdom, including Swindon, Aldershot, Wembley, Bradford, Yarmouth (non League), Bristol, Wolverhampton, Neath, St.Austell, and Glasgow.

On 20 September 1966, Trevor introduced the European Formula 2 Stock Car Championship Final to Par Moor. This was the first time it was held in the region. Another motorsport achievement for T.R.

It was Johnny Marquand (no.189) who won the event. In the same year, T.R. sold White City Speedway Stadium to Les Whaley.

In September 1968, Trevor brought the Super Hot Rod World Championship to Newton Abbott. Winner of this spectacular class of racing was John Harris of Exeter. Within a couple of year's T.R. teamed up with Bernard Cottrell and achieved what seemed like the impossible to many by reintroducing speedway to the Empire Stadium at Wembley. He appointed former Wembley teamster Freddie Williams as his team manager. The ebullient and eternally cheerful T.R. presented the first speedway at Wembley for thirteen years. Wembley won their first home league meeting against Hackney. Trevor said at that time, "For years I wanted to bring back speedway to Wembley. We had talks with them every year or two just to keep in touch and this year everything seemed to be right to bring it back."

T.R.s big coup was to bring speedway champion Ove Fundin into spearhead 'The Lions'. Trevor praised the champion by saying, "I'm fortunate that Ove is a great friend. He has often been to my place and I've stayed with him in Sweden, we have also toured together. This is just the right man to lead Wembley."

A crowd of over 20,000 watched Wembley quickly settle down on a newly laid track. Bengt Jansson recorded the fastest time of the night. Ove Fundin was unbeaten but excluded from his third ride for breaking the tapes. Wayne Briggs, who rode at the St.Austell track as a teenager, gave team-mate Fundin some solid support. With only four points separating the teams, Hackney certainly gave the League newcomers some spirited opposition.

Bill Dalley who was Trevor's regular announcer at St.Austell, Neath and even for a short time at Weymouth recalled his first time at Wembley. T.R. had paid Bob Danvers Walker, the voice of radio to do his commentaries. Well he did a smashing job talking about the history of Wembley because it had all been written down for him. When it came to the 'speedway commentary' Bob started to falter a bit. Wembley Lions were pitched against Wimbledon Dons. The Dons won the match. In the second half racing several former World Champion's including Barry Briggs and Ronnie Moore were invited to take part in match races. Bob Danvers Walker uncharacteristically faltered again at the microphone.

T.R. by this time had lost his cool and came storming up the track, shouting "Bill, Bill, for God's sake get that ------ off the microphone." Trevor brought in Radio disc jockey Ed 'Stewpot' Stewart who was an immediate success with younger fans having hosted 'Junior Choice.'

In 1971, T.R.'s regular announcer at 'Lions' home meetings was Martin Rogers. T.R. had a major influence on Martin at this time and nudged him towards promoting. Today the former speedway boss of Leicester, Kings Lynn and Peterborough lives on Queensland's beautiful Gold Coast. He said, "Trevor Redmond made speedway fun, he promoted with a smile, he could talk the talk, considered every occasion special and every rider someone."

Not many people may realise but it was T.R. who also introduced 'Banger racing' to the South-West region. He invited a small group of amateur drivers to compete against one another. They were not skilful with their driving technique and kept on bumping or scraping one another. Trevor's face lit up, "Why didn't I think of that before," he exclaimed, "We'll call it Bangers and Smash." Soon this form of motor sport became a regular feature at Cornish Stadium, Ringwood, Weymouth, Newton Abbot, and at United Downs near St.Day.

In 1969, Bill Batten (no.651) made his racing debut driving at Cornish Stadium. Bill would go on to be the World, European, and British Stock Car 'title holder' and the sport's most successful driver.

With a slump in car racing in the early seventies Trevor Redmond spent somewhere in the region of £2,000 to give Cornish Stadium 'a bit of a make over.' In 1972, he put on the World Stock Car Final at Par Moor. This was the first time the final had ever been held so far west. Part of the revamp included some bench seating and a windbreak. The event was heralded as a huge success and brought in a crowd of 12,000 people. This was the same volume of spectators the Luke family had through the turnstiles to open the stadium in 1949.

Cornish Stadium was the setting for the 'Bangers and Crash World Championship Final' in August 1973. Believe it or not, 101 cars started the event.Bob Higgins won the 'manic meeting' receiving prize money of £100. In June 1974 T.R. took the Formula 2 World Stock Car Final to Wembley. He had support racing from Formula 1 stocks and again enjoyed the fruits of his labours. Trevor loved to put on a good show, it was serious but still like a game to him! Hence, he latched onto doing very visual things. When his wife Pat ran a confectionery business Trevor gave out 'gigantic' chocolate Easter eggs as prizes. Some sceptics have claimed they were never eaten but this isn't true, one year he broke up a huge egg and went amongst the crowd giving chocolate to the children. Trevor was noted for giving away free Cornish pasties too!

With Trevor being so involved with three tracks, St.Austell, Newton Abbot, and St.Day, sometimes there was an overlap with times of meetings. This meant his regular commentator Bill Dalley had to travel to Newton Abbott while Trevor filled the spot on the microphone at Par Moor. This is briefly the story of when a car caught fire. Unbeknown to Trevor he didn't realise the microphone wasn't turned off. He just blurted out, "Leave the car burn, give the crowd some spectacle."

In August 1974, Trevor brought the 'World Production Car and Banger's Hurly Burly' to Newton Abbot. Spence Morgan won ahead of Alan Murton. The following season Autospeed introduced a new formula for Jaguars. The big saloons proved popular, yet another success for T.R. Two years later Trevor promoted the Westward Television Grand Prix Series. Racing took part across the region, which was broadcast to South-West television viewers. The tracks at St.Day, St.Austell, Newton Abbot, Smeartharpe and Mendips all saw action. Bill Batten was the overall winner of the series bagging 149 points.

A person who knew Trevor better than most was Neil Truran who worked as his caretaker at Par Moor in 1977. Neil's family were involved in providing 'the fast food catering' at the circuit for many years. T.R. gave Neil several litres of paint to freshen up the deteriorating sheeting and bar area. Neil rang Trevor at home to explain he was 'running out of paint', Trevor said, "Water it down a bit". Neil protested by saying he had already watered it down. Trevor retorted, "Well water it down a bit more Neil, you'll have to make do!" Incidentally Neil Truran has raced almost everything on four wheels and usually had some success. Many will remember Neil (no.306) blazing to the chequered flag in National Stock Rods. Today he still fondly displays a picture of Cornish Stadium in his office.

Trevor remained keen on speedway and continued to manage the New Zealand National Speedway Team. Ivan Mauger M.B.E. said, 'Trevor was indeed proud of his roots.' We must never forget Trevor of course helped many great riders like Martin Ashby, Charlie Monk, Jon Erskine, and George Major grab a foothold in the sport. He also brought over South African Howdy Cornell.

Crispen Rosevear, who went on to become Trevor's Autospeed Racing manager gave an example of Trevor's 'gaming about.' On 6 April 1980, a local guy named Mike Nancekivell (no.553), a giant of a man at 6' 7" tall won the Stock car event at St.Day. Trevor said to Mike, "We'll need the trophy back for engraving." What Trevor had handed Mike was the 'World Speedway Team Cup.' This was the team trophy that had been previously won by the New Zealand aces. Mike was having none of it. Trevor gave in and bought Mike a new trophy for winning his event that afternoon.

In 1979, Trevor put on the World Championship Brisca Formula 2 Stock Car Final at Newton Abbot. In that year it was won by Dave Brown, who became the first triple winner of the title.

A typical T.R. story which highlights the showman again was the probably the only ever appearance of the Irish champion at Par Moor. For his reasons Jeremy is not going to name the persons involved but the gist of the tale was as follows. T.R. paid the local Super Hot Rod driver some money to get his car resprayed green and gold. He was asked to change his number from 6 to 246. All the billboard and advertising carried the details of Number 246, they all said Danny O'Shea the Irish Champion was making his first appearance at Par Moor. A small minority in the pits knew Danny didn't exist but the majority of the visitors to the venue didn't know. Today it is unlikely this prank would take place due to changes in insurance liability and tougher legislation.

August Bank Holiday Monday 1987 saw the final racing at Par Moor. Trevor-could not re-negotiate a deal to secure further racing at the venue. Sadly, it lay dormant for some time before it was redeveloped. The last meeting included Bangers, Super-rods, Saloon Stocks, and the final appearance of the sidecar speedway outfits.

Jerry Rundle won the last 'Destruction Derby' held at the track and took the chequered flag home with him.

In 1983, the World Stock Car Championship Final again came to Devon.

It was Dave Bunt who held the trophy aloft at Newton Abbot. Into the nineties T.R. was getting older but still didn't relish retiring. He provided us with many wise words regarding young people starting in the sport. Trevor said, "It is okay to install enthusiasm into children to take part but it is something else when parents try to live through their children."

In the mid-nineties Westworld Raceway at Retallack Park near St.Columb Major staged national stock racing for the first time, thanks to Trevor's efforts.

Today Westworld is billed 'The Cornish Stadium' but for those of us who are nostalgic about Par Moor, it will never be quite that.

Trevor Redmond was one of the guests at the White Gold Classic and Custom Bike Show in 1994. Here he is being caught by former track pushers Geoff Jarvis and Mickey Luxon for ten shillings (50 pence) they reckoned T.R. each owed them from 1963. T.R. of course paid in full!

A few mistakes had been made in the programmes over the years but it didn't matter, because T.R. had in the main given great entertainment and proved to all he was indeed a showman, probably the last of them! The late Eddie Seymour, the distinguished commentator once fittingly described Trevor as 'a folk legend'.

Trevor continued with his car racing interests up to his untimely death. As a fitting memorial to T.R. an award named the Trevor Redmond Trophy was presented at Ringwood raceway in November 2002. The bronze award shaped just like T.R.s trilby hat was presented to driver Eddie Darby who had become the first South West driver to win the Saloon Stock Car British Championship in Scotland. The hat is awarded annually to the driver in the 'Autospeed family' who has produced the most magnificent result throughout the season.

Westcountry speedway fans are lucky because T.R.s influence rubbed off on

Brian Annear who was the innovator and builder of the Claycountry Moto-Parc. The racing at the circuit in the confines of an old clay pit produced some memorable nights. Sadly, the track no longer exists as it was reclaimed by the landowners, china clay giants Imerys. Today Cornwall has no speedway track but the fans are ever hopeful it will return one day. Until that time comes, we will have to content ourselves with the knowledge that as spectator's we have seen so much good racing down the years. As for the guys who enjoy the four-wheeled sport in the Westcountry they will all have some memory of T.R. It is uncanny though how his eldest son Guy has taken to talking on a microphone, in the couple of years that he and his mother Pat flew the 'Autospeed flag' after T.R.s death, 'a chip off the old block if ever I saw one!'

Finally Trevor Redmond would never believe what speedway enthusiasts today will pay at auctions or online for 'Neath Abbey Welsh Dragons' or 'St. Austell Gulls' lapel badges, and even race programmes made famous of course by T.R. all those years ago! Without a shadow of doubt Trevor Redmond over the years brought many happy times and memorable nights for thousands of motorsport enthusiasts. Through this achievement alone 'his memory will live on.'